RUNNING YOUR OWN BUSINESS

RUNNING YOUR OWN BUSINESS

NEW, REVISED, UPDATED EDITION

A HANDBOOK OF FACTS AND INFORMATION

Howard H. Stern

INTRODUCTION BY LAURENCE J. PETER,
AUTHOR OF THE PETER PRINCIPLE

CROWN PUBLISHERS, INC.
NEW YORK

To
my lovely and loving wife, Marcia,
who handled all the difficult tasks
while I wrote this book

Published by Crown Publishers, Inc.,
225 Park Avenue South, New York, New York 10003
and simultaneously in Canada
by General Publishing Company Limited
Manufactured in the United States of America
CROWN is a trademark of Crown Publishers, Inc.

Library of Congress Cataloging in Publication Data

Stern, Howard H.
Running your own business.

1. Small business—Management—Handbooks, manuals,
etc.   2. Business—Handbooks, manuals, etc.

I. Title.
HD62.7.S815 1986   658'.022   85-9661

ISBN 0-517-558203
10 9 8 7 6 5 6 4 3 2 1
First Revised Edition

CONTENTS

PREFACE

This book is a primer for the businessman, particularly the small businessman. It contains information on every aspect of business operation, concentrating on how to effectively handle almost any situation that might occur in running a business. Because my objective was to cram as much practical information into as few pages as possible, I have deliberately left out background theory and explanations. Instead, I drew on my own observations and experience, augmented with technical information from many sources. In reaching my conclusions, I have relied on my own judgment, and although my opinions cannot be tested by a rigorous proof, I believe they are right anyway.

In reading the book—a few cautions. First, depending on whether it is used in an accounting or an operational sense, the definition of *sales* changes. You should, however, be able to shift gears when the occasion demands and apply the meaning that suits the context. In addition, *product* and *service* overlap in meaning. I ended up using *product* for the true services of the business entity, even if the output was an intangible. Finally, because I do not consider myself sufficiently knowledgeable about the subject, I have not discussed taxes at all, and you should consult an expert in that area. I do hope, however, that after you apply the principles on these pages, taxes are your only problem.

INTRODUCTION

BY DR. LAURENCE J. PETER

Why did Howard Stern wait so long before writing this book? I needed it six years ago when I found myself at a new level of incompetence. After teaching for over thirty years I quit my job as a university professor to take up writing as a full-time job. The transition from teaching to writing presented few problems. Authoring successful manuscripts presented no insurmountable difficulties. Six of my books and many of my articles have been published during the six years since I resigned from teaching.

In 1970, for the first time in my professional career, I was really my own boss. I had the full responsibility of determining what I was going to do as well as when and where to do it. In the beginning I maintained an office away from home. I soon discovered that this office provided facilities that were easily duplicated at home, commuting was wasted time, and that the flow of ideas essential to a writer did not operate on a nine-to-five schedule. Within a few months the office in town was abandoned and a spare bedroom was converted into a combined study and office. I soon realized that the book author was engaged in one of the few remaining cottage industries in America. The author had to deal directly, or through agents, with publishers and contract to provide an acceptable manuscript. From that point on the writing of the manuscript was completely in the author's hands.

But the relatively simple task of writing marketable manuscripts was only a small part of the business of being an author. In thinking about the business of writing I asked myself some questions. How does a writer support his family during the no-income years of research and development of a manuscript? As a beginner, can he obtain an adequate advance? After the manuscript is completed, what does he live on during the year in which his manuscript is being transformed into a published book? How does he get by until his first royalty check arrives? The chance that his royalty check will be substantial is extremely remote. Over 30,000 books are published each year but only a few become best-sellers.

I thought about this strange business I was in. One triumph does not make a successful career. Much that constitutes success is pure chance. Popular taste could change faster than I can write. Considering the time lapse between finished manuscript and printed book, it is simple luck if the mood of the public coincides with my subject matter and the publication date. How does the author maintain a lifetime income in this feast and famine business? I am essentially in a business of wasting assets. Every idea I use is one less idea I retain. I do not have the tax advantages granted the petroleum industry. The IRS does not grant me a Brain Depletion Allowance. Inevitably my inspiration will be depleted, whether early in my new career or later on as senility approaches.

As each problem in my writing business was resolved, another appeared. No longer an employee eligible for a pension, how and when should I plan to retire? No longer a member of a group, what medical coverage could I obtain or afford? As a self-employed author are my sick-pay and holidays-with-pay a thing of the past? As management I wanted sound fiscal planning and as labor I wanted all the benefits I could get.

For me the adjustments in lifestyle and working conditions required by the shift from teaching to writing were insignificant compared to those imposed by the move from being an employee to being self-employed. In describing my experiences, frustrations, and problems in running my own little writing business I spared you the sordid details of the mistakes I made on my own and the bad "expert" advice I followed. In spite of the mistakes and added risks and responsibilities I have experienced more of the joy of accomplishment in the past six years than in the previous thirty.

In relating my story of how I left teaching, a profession I loved, and became a self-employed author, a profession full of imponderables, I do not intend to imply that your business is like mine. But my observations indicate that many intelligent, professionally or technically competent individuals, in their respective fields, have difficulties in running their own businesses because of lack of knowledge of the specific procedures required. How is a fallible human being, alone, or with the help of others who are equally fallible, going to run a business and cope with constantly changing circumstances and come out a winner?

In running your own business there are no theories that will solve your problems—there are only actions, either intelligent, not-too-bright, or stupid. It is easy to identify these types of actions. The intelligent ones are eminently successful while the not-too-bright actions produce questionable results and the stupid actions end up in disasters.

Success may be elusive, but intelligent action will improve your chances of achieving success. This book tells you what you need to know about your own abilities, what you have to know about your personal characteristics and what you need to know about business practices. This knowledge will place you well ahead of most who try to run their own businesses. To start with, one should not imitate the model established by big business. Frequently, big business is not as efficient as its admirers would like you to believe. Furthermore, very few small businesses are eligible for taxpayer funding to the degree that Litton Industries, General Electric, Lockheed, General Dynamics, or other biggies are accustomed. In most cases, the small independent business must make it on its own.

The rationality presented in *Running Your Own Business* provides the most promising approach even though many successful executives appear to be lacking in rationality. Where I live the manager of a local gourmet restaurant eats regularly at a fast-food chain outlet across the street. Howard Hughes gave generously to medical research but personally suffered from medical neglect. The chairman of the English-owned Cunard Line never took a ship to America. It seems that some successful business leaders are eccentric to the point of lunacy, but interesting as their idiosyncratic methods are, the potential businessman and struggling business owner is well advised to rely on a more straightforward or logical approach. Copying the behavior of eccentrics seldom pays off. On the other hand, if you are a genuine oddball the reasonable procedures described in this book will have limited appeal. So, read on. Nothing ventured, nothing gained. If you decide against going into your own business, nothing ventured, nothing lost.

1
WHAT IS IT ALL ABOUT, ANYWAY?

When small businessmen are asked what it is they want from their companies they answer, as if on cue, "Profits."

They might have given the answer they thought was wanted. Perhaps they were kidding themselves. They may have read too many business magazines and developed conditioned responses.

The truth is that most of them were lying.

A goodly number had some inner compulsion to prove themselves or to show someone else.

Some businesses came into being because the owner could not hold a job and had to find some way to earn a living.

People with inherited money often have companies to keep themselves occupied.

I know one man who started his business to give himself an excuse for getting away from the wife and kiddies. I suspect a couple more.

Another wanted a base of operations for his true avocation, politics.

Many use their businesses as security blankets.

An admirable few employ them to help others.

Some like being a father figure to their employees.

And then there are those people who start companies to profit from the things they enjoy doing. In this enviable category are boatyard owners, bush pilots, tennis pros, ski instructors, and band leaders.

Bigger is not necessarily better. A business is best when it suits your needs. Nobody can argue with that.

There is one small problem, however. Businesses do not survive unless they take in more than they put out. To keep your business plugging along you need those profits you give lip service to. At least enough to cushion the bad years. That is what this book is about.

What you ask for is what you get

The owner who used his business to help his political career was out of town too often. Unable to get decisions from an absentee owner, the employees lost interest. The owner's political influence went bankrupt along with the business.

Two of the father figures I am familiar with were so paternalistic they turned employees into helpless children. Employees who maintained their independence and initiative eventually quit. Both owners lost their companies to disenchanted investors.

An extraordinarily talented builder who always had plenty of work never earned enough to build a home of his own. He was a perfectionist and let economics take second place to the appearance of the homes he built. This was a windfall for his clients, but it did not do his family much good.

You must know where you are headed

A business can be a personal possession or a means of acquiring wealth. When you start out you must decide which, because it is not easy to change later on.

If you want to parlay your company into great capital gains you must think about going public or selling out to a large corporation someday. That means you must produce large profits. The price of your company, whether to another company or to the public, is determined by the earnings it shows in its audited financial statement.

And if you plan on going public your statements must be audited by a certified public accountant for three years (or every year from inception if your company is less than three years old). Otherwise you cannot qualify for a full-blown registration of your stock. Your company may be a world-beater and the new-issue market may be at an all-time high, but if you stinted on last year's financial statement you are out of luck.

On the other hand, if you want a personal kind of business, who needs earnings? Earnings are something to pay income taxes on. And accountants are people who make out your tax return if you can't handle it yourself.

The two are not the same, so make up your mind early.

What you put in

Anyone who has his own business can tell you. The hours are long and the possession possesses. You are never really away from it. You must work hard, know a lot, ward off disappointments, rally the troops, and make that ultimate decision. The buck stops with you. Explanations and excuses are meaningless. The condition of your company says it all.

What you need

- To run your own business you need a product or a service (or an idea for one).
- Some knowledge of what you are doing.
- Money. Probably more than you have.
- A plan.
- T & P (tenacity and perseverance).
- It also helps to know something about yourself.

Some businesses do not make it

The bankruptcy and failure rate of businesses has always been very high. Only about one-third of all retail establishments last through the fifth year. Extremes in the economic climate, like high inflation, aggravate the failure rates.

The biggest causes of failures are poor management and undercapitalization. Disputes between partners cause many failures, but this is because of the resulting poor management.

Another cause is that the owner quits too soon; he does not have T & P.

You should plan to make it

If you have your own business, plan it to be successful. Believe in it. Act like you believe in it. Talk like you believe in it. But do not let that stop you from taking precautions, because there will be times when it seems like the whole world is geared to stop you.

Think positive but protect your flanks.

2

SHAPING UP

STRUCTURE

Legal form

Companies are usually classified as sole proprietorships, partnerships, or corporations. There are other forms, such as joint ventures and cooperatives, but these will not be covered here.

The difference between the three major categories lies primarily in the liability of the owners, the survivability of the entity, and the manner in which it is taxed.

Sole proprietorship

A sole proprietorship can be equated with self-employment. The assets of the business and of the owner are commingled. Unsatisfied personal creditors can attach business assets and business creditors may look to personal assets. If an employee of the company, acting in an official capacity, commits a tort against a customer, the owner's personal fortune is jeopardized.

The earnings of the business are the personal earnings of the owner. It does not matter what form these earnings take (cash, capital equipment, inventory, or accounts receivable). The owner pays income tax on the company's profit, regardless. If the company's profit went into a new building with fancy equipment, the owner must pay the taxes in cash, even if he has to borrow to do so.

When a proprietor dies his business may have to be liquidated to pay estate taxes or to settle the claims of the heirs.

Businesses are most likely to be sole proprietorships when they are new. Tax consequences are not taken into account when earnings are low, and the threat of personal liability is not felt very strongly when all of the owner's assets are represented by the business. When the business matures and the owner acquires a new home and starts his financial portfolio, he takes a closer look at the advantages of incorporating.

Partnership

A partnership is an agreement between two or more parties to conduct a business for profit. Each partner shares in the revenues or losses to the extent that is stated in the agreement. Partners are taxed on all the earnings of the company, pro rata. To that extent it is similar to the proprietorship.

A partnership is a very dangerous business form because of the personal liabilities of each partner. Not only is he liable to the full extent of his personal assets for his own actions and the actions of the partnership but he is liable also for the acts of each and every partner.

A 10-percent partner is liable to outside creditors for 100 percent of the company's obligations. If one partner absconds with a client's funds, the other may have to make restitution out of his personal holdings. No wonder that professional partnerships changed to corporations in such large numbers once the law made it possible.

Limited partnership

Investors can be limited partners, not subject to the liabilities of general partners, so long as their only involvement is financial and they have no say in running the business. Regardless of limited partnership agreements, if you happen to be the only partner with personal wealth, any attorney suing the partnership will try to show that you were a general partner in fact if not in name. If he succeeds, you are hooked. Be careful of limited partnerships. Lawyers always go after the guy with money. This is called the *deep pockets* principle.

Corporation

A corporation is a legal entity created by the state. It has many of the rights and obligations of a person, including the right to sue and be sued. Ownership of a corporation is held by stockholders, that is, the people who finance the company by buying stock certificates. By selling their certificates, stockholders may sell their ownership without affecting the operation of the corporation. The certificate is not in itself an equity right, it is only a representation of ownership. The actual owners are those persons listed as stockholders on the books of the corporation. A person does not obtain ownership rights by finding or stealing a stock certificate. Conversely, a stockholder whose certificate is lost or stolen can get it replaced by the corporation.

Limited liability

Stockholders are not liable for the acts of the corporation or for the acts of any of the employees, officers, or directors of the corporation. Creditors and wronged parties can sue the corporation and attach assets of the corporation but have no course of action against the shareholders. Owners can therefore limit the amount of wealth they put at risk and protect assets held outside the corporation.

Perpetual life

When a partner dies the partnership is dissolved. When a stockholder dies, the corporation goes on as before. To pay estate taxes the heirs may have to sell some of their shares of stock, but there is no need to liquidate the business. Furthermore, the estate can be broken into many parts without severing the business.

Corporate taxes

Corporate taxation is complex, and stockholder-employees are taxed at several levels. The corporation pays state and federal income taxes on its earnings. The stockholder pays personal income tax on his salary and on any dividends he receives. If a stockholder-employee receives a high salary, the IRS may declare part of that salary to be dividends, because salary is a business expense and therefore deductable from corporate income, whereas dividends are not.

If this sounds confusing, it is only the start. Tax advice is not part of this book, so as soon as your corporation starts earning profits get the help of a competent tax accountant. Nobody has the time to run a business and keep up with the tax regulations.

Subchapter S corporation

Small groups can form a special type of corporation that has most of the characteristics of a general corporation but is treated like a partnership or proprietorship for tax purposes. It is slanted toward professional groups like lawyers and physicians, but other types of businesses may choose it also. The major advantage is that it protects the participator from liability resulting from torts caused by other members of the corporation. For example, a malpractice claim against one doctor in a Subchapter S corporation cannot be pursued against the personal wealth of the other doctors, as it could be in a partnership.

Forming a corporation

It is a relatively simple operation to form a corporation, and the costs will not be high unless the capitalization is substantial. A state charter must be applied for, taxes and fees paid, corporate bylaws and articles drawn up and filed, stock issued, and directors elected. The directors then elect the officers who run the company on a day-by-day basis.

The task is elementary and is handled primarily by the secretary of a lawyer practicing business law. Fees should be minimal. Get several quotes from attorneys in your city.

Warning

Sometimes owners think that by forming a corporation they can escape responsibility for improper acts. This is not true.

Any employee who commits a tort can be sued along with the corporation. As the owner and president you can bet you will not be overlooked by the plaintiff's attorney.

Incorporating does protect you from improper acts of other employees, however, and that is worth a lot.

ORGANIZING

If your company has more than one employee the work must be divided in some manner. You could tell the additional person what to do or you could tell him what he is responsible for and let him decide what to do. If you choose the latter course you have created an organization. The more employees you add, the more necessary it is to define duties and therefore the more formal the organization must be.

While your company is small you should organize the work load in a way that best suits the talents and the personalities of the people, including yourself. As it grows in size the organization must become more structured and should follow conventional lines, because you must know who is in charge of the various functions and your employees or managers must be able to interact with one another without too much confusion. The organization should never become so rigid that it cannot be modified to meet special circumstances. Employees should have a little leeway to do their job in an unorthodox manner.

Organize for results

The largest corporation has this in common with a one-man shop: the number of things it does. All there is to business is produce and sell. Other activities support or evaluate the produce-sell functions. The company should therefore be organized to do the best possible job of making and selling.

Company roles

Do not become confused by your employees' views of the job functions.

Accountants do not create profits. They record profits. A good accountant will prevent the salesman from selling quantities that are too small or will show a manufacturing man how to reduce costs, but the profit still comes from selling for a higher price than the service costs.

An engineer's business purpose is not to design, it is to help produce and help sell. In a company whose product is design or engineering services, the engineer is actually both the producer and the salesman. The fact that the engineer spends most of his time designing is only incidental.

Inspectors do not impart quality to the product, they find defects. Quality is put in by the workman who builds the product or by the engineer who decides how it is to be built. The inspector helps them to do a better job.

Ways to organize

Suppose your business is cutting and sewing shirts for Sears and Penney. You have two employees, Mary and Ruth.

Suppose you put Mary in charge of cutting and Ruth in charge of sewing. You have created a functional or horizontal organization. Mary and Ruth work for both customers but they divide the operations.

If you put Mary in charge of Sears and Ruth in charge of Penney, you have created a project or vertical organization. Mary and Ruth perform both functions but they divvy up the customers.

You could have two products, shirts and blouses, and divide the work by product line. This is a product organization, which is also vertical.

Every organization is a combination of horizontal and vertical structuring.

Advantages and disadvantages of functional organization

A functional organization is versatile. It can handle a large number of different jobs for different customers. It is efficient because the people perform, all the time, the tasks they do best.

Its weakness lies in communications and control. Jobs often get mixed up; they are difficult to schedule and hard to find. There is also a tendency for overspecialization to demotivate employees.

As companies grow in the number of products they produce, there is a need to break up functional organizations along product lines. If the only thing that increases as the company grows is the size of the orders, the functional system works even better.

Vertical organization

Vertical organizations provide tight control and good communications. Their disadvantage is in duplication, because every function must be repeated for each product or project. There is little standardization, and the efficiencies inherent in doing the same thing many times are lost.

Another weakness is that projects die slowly and the best people are kept on them until the very end.

Because of inefficiencies, vertical organizations are rarely used until they are large enough to be independent horizontal organizations.

Task force

When a particularly important job must be performed in a horizontal organization, people are pulled together from different functional groups and formed into a team. This is often very successful, because the best people are chosen and working together they usually develop a special esprit de corps. There is a law of diminishing returns related to task forces, however. The more that are created at any one time, the less effective they become.

Matrix

Large companies combine the vertical and horizontal organizations into a matrix system. This is done by setting up two distinct organizations and giving them conflicting responsibilities for the same tasks. The functional group strives to do the best job overall, and the product or project group sees that their customer or product gets sufficient attention.

The three-legged stool

To maintain balance it is advisable to have the departments responsible for selling, measuring, and producing at the same level. Other departments can report there as well, but no less than marketing (or sales), manufacturing (or operations), and accounting (or finance) should report to the manager responsible for the profit or loss.

What is balance?

Dividing a company into organizations has a valuable side effect. In addition to defining responsibilities it creates conflict. Conflict is the best thing that ever happens to a manager, because it provides him with insight and with options. A company is balanced when the key departments fight on equal terms. Because a manager must apportion his resources between making and selling, he needs conflict. The financial man is there to appraise and contradict the statements of the other two, as well as to find outside funds when desirable. Is finding outside funds a fourth function of a business? Or is it simply supporting the make-sell function? Even though I hold the latter view, there is no doubt that the financial leg of the stool must be as long as the other two.

LOCATION AND PLANT

In addition to being structured from a legal standpoint and organized from a personnel standpoint, your business obviously must be situated physically. Different businesses require different locations and different kinds of buildings. Here are the factors that must be considered in choosing your physical surroundings.

Location

- Nearness to markets
- Nearness to suppliers
- Availability of labor

- Cost of utilities
- Availability of transportation
- Tax benefits
- Attitude of the community
- Cost of land
- Stability of the neighborhood
- Safety
- Insurance rates

During the late seventies, residential housing costs became a prime factor in the selection of plant locations. Expansion into Silicon Valley (Santa Clara, California) slowed down for this reason more than any other. New employees were difficult to obtain because they could not afford the local housing.

When the management of General Dynamics decided that their New York City location no longer was suitable for corporate headquarters, they instituted an exhaustive study of possible new locations. Where did they finally move? To St. Louis, where the chief executive had his home.

That's not such a bad idea. Be sure to locate your business near where you enjoy living.

Building

Building or buying a new plant takes much work and careful planning. You must consider people needs and functional needs. You must consult with many of your employees. Unfortunately, this can result in petty conflicts as people vie for the best offices and the most space for their departments. Keep the discussions going until you have little more to learn, then set the ground rules. Let everyone know that their inputs were considered but that compromise was unavoidable.

Here are items which must be reviewed without haste:

- Appearance
- Layout
- Cost

- Lighting
- Shipping facilities
- Power
- Parking
- Acoustics
- Water
- Waste disposal
- Safety
- Comfort

3

HOW DO YOU STACK UP
AS A MANAGER?

In the early 1950s Donald Douglas, Jr., son of the founder of Douglas Aircraft Company, appeared on the Groucho Marx television show. When Groucho learned that his guest was vice-president of the company he said with that famous sneer, "I don't suppose your being Donald Douglas's son had anything to do with that?"

"No, Groucho, as a matter of fact it didn't," the young man replied. I was watching the show at the time, and I thought that was one of the funniest lines ever dropped on television. The poor fellow actually had come to believe that he had worked his way up to vice-president on his merits. I decided then that anyone so susceptible to self-delusion would not make a good chief executive.

The moral of the story is to understand yourself and have no illusions about why you are where you are. A manager with known weaknesses can very easily bolster them.

How good do you have to be?

Almost anyone can start a business and run it with modest success if he selects a business that does not overstress his abilities. If you start off with enough wealth and are lucky enough to hire the right people, success may be possible in any field.

So, to some extent, how good you have to be depends upon how well you know yourself. The more inflated your self-image is and the fewer doubts you have, the better you must *really* be. It is a shame that a majority of people who start businesses are so self-confident. Many succeed at first because of their ego and later fail because of that very weakness. Those people who have too many self-doubts to start their own company may in the long run be better qualified to be in charge.

What qualities must a manager have?

A manager's personal assets fall into four categories: his character, his knowledge, his intelligence, and his talent. Of these, I believe character is the most important, although one cannot be bereft of knowledge and intelligence.

Talent is something else. With enough talent you can call the shots. A skillful inventor can insist upon being president of someone else's company, and he may get takers. Mohammad Ali ran a very successful enterprise with the talent in his fists.

Surgeons, artists, artisans, athletes, entertainers, and innovators succeed on their talents. Most businessmen, lacking such gifts, succeed by their intelligence, acquired knowledge, determination, toughness, energy, and plain luck. Few will be able to match in a lifetime the success of some talented rock stars in their twenties.

Character

A manager must have tenacity and perseverance, because success does not come quickly and failure is often a state of mind.

A manager must be objective, because the outside world does not adjust itself to his preconceptions.

A manager must listen carefully, because his subordinates will often adjust their words to fit his preconceptions.

A manager must be fair to his customers and to his employees.

A manager must know what he wants even if he does not know how to get it.

16

A manager must be capable of making decisions and be capable of delegating authority.

Personality blocks

Most managers have a high degree of emotional direction. They do things out of compulsion rather than reason. At a critical moment these emotions can betray them.

Some managers cannot wait to make decisions, others put them off until it is too late. Some managers delegate nothing, others everything. Many go off half-cocked at the first hint of a problem and berate some innocent subordinate. Others fear to criticize even when it is deserved. These are all compulsive traits.

If you have such a compulsion, beware. It is your greatest enemy.

The tin ear

The most common compulsive trait of entrepreneurs is inability to listen. Suggestions that come to the manager from employees, associates, or outsiders are invariably discarded without consideration, not because the manager is unable to understand or evaluate but because he never takes the trouble to listen.

The strange part of this phenomenon is that such a person may be able to reply to the question without having heard it. In fact, he may have trained himself to answer it politely as if he were grateful for the suggestion. It is all sham.

If you have such a trait, you are probably aware of it. Force yourself to listen. Your success depends more on keeping your ears and mind open than on any other single factor. When somebody suggests something to you, ask yourself three questions:

- What did he say?
- Is he right?
- Does it mean anything?

Pay no attention to who said it or to the surrounding circumstances. It may have been said by someone you consider stupid or it may have been intended to embarrass you. Neither makes a difference. If it is right, accept it. If it means anything, act on it.

Infallibility syndrome

It is easy to see how this can come about. After a string of early successes an entrepreneur comes to believe, sometimes correctly, that he has a special talent or sixth sense that is unique. His subordinates support this opinion with acquiescence or flattery so that he comes to believe his every utterance is correct. I call this sometimes fatal disease *executive infallibility*. You all know people who suffer from it. Many will lose their businesses hanging on to their mistakes, thinking that they have been betrayed by their employees. The syndrome can be overcome only by failure, so the cure is worse than the disease. Prevention may be possible if you are aware of its existence and take steps to avoid it. Remember, people may agree with you because of your position and in spite of your logic.

Knowledge

There are two kinds of knowledge you can obtain. Knowledge from books and knowledge from experience. Both are important. The knowledge you gain from experience allows you to apply the book knowledge to your particular business.

Experience provides you with information about the way things are done in your industry and it teaches you about people. Its value is underrated by the young and overrated by the mature.

How much of a manager's knowledge is transferable? Is a good manager capable of running any business? Not until he learns the ways of that industry.

Intelligence

A manager must be intelligent enough to resolve conflicts, to establish priorities, to make fundamental decisions, and to maintain the respect of his employees. He does not have to be capable of understanding complicated technical matters. If he is running a highly technical company, he should have some grasp of the technical implications of his decisions. He should not be in a business where the day-to-day activities are beyond his comprehension.

Ability to communicate

A manager should strive to communicate with his employees, but even more important, he must encourage communications by his employees, among themselves.

If you are a poor communicator, expose yourself often enough to give your subordinates a chance to drag information out of you. That is the least you can do. Hold staff meetings and encourage questions.

What does a manager do, anyway?

There is one thing you must do; hire your key employees. After that it is really your choice. How much you do will depend upon how much time you have available. So one of your prime work disciplines is time management. You must be sure to do all of the important things that you have taken on for yourself. Among your highest-priority items are these:

- Establishing objectives
- Selecting markets and products
- Creating the character of the company
- Motivating key employees
- Setting the business attitude
- Evaluating progress, rewarding and criticizing
- Providing direction
- Resolving conflicts
- Representing the company in the financial community

If your company is small but adequately manned there will be time for you to do other things. This extra time can be the undoing of your business because it may get you involved in the day-to-day business cycle to the extent that you are unable to handle your primary tasks. You may also demotivate personnel by interfering in their jobs.

You can do some things safely, however, like reviewing plans and finding loopholes. You can help with the selling effort. You can compile information about your business, your competition, and your market. You can work on new products, provided you are not too disruptive. Whatever you undertake, however, you must be able to drop at a moment's notice for a high-priority activity.

Decision making

The hardest part about making a decision is recognizing when one has to be made. That is why you must foster conflict. Your employees must bring their unresolved disputes to you, together with the facts and the logic of their arguments. This is the greatest tool a decision maker can have.

Setting the attitude

To create argumentative employees you must establish the proper climate in your company. People must be deprived of any protective rights to their territory. No one must be permitted the right to say to another, "That's my business, stay out of it." Questions should be encouraged. Disputes should be treated as part of the normal course of business, not as matters of grave concern. No one should be praised for winning an argument or berated for being on the wrong side. Employees' only concern should be about the results the company achieves and the manner in which they have contributed.

Build on your strengths

Everyone has areas of strength. As a manager you should learn to utilize your strengths in new, managerial ways. If you are a skilled engineer, learn how to use this skill to predict market opportunities rather than to design equipment. If you are an accomplished accountant, set the plans for establishing a strong financial base for the company instead of keeping the books.

Shore up your weaknesses

If you are not good at something, do not fake it. Learn what to do or get someone else to handle it. If you can't sell, don't try. That's what you have salesmen for. If you cannot understand accounting or engineering, make it the accountant's job or the engineer's job to present information in a way you can understand. Be quick to call in your experts when a conversation gets over your head.

RECAPPING THE CHAPTER

Do not feel frightened if you feel inadequate at times. You probably are doing better than a lot of know-it-alls. Learn to pick good people, treat them fairly, and keep an open mind and an attentive ear. Use your common sense and keep striving. You will get there.

4

LOOKING AHEAD

PLANNING

Planning is the act of determining the future actions required to reach a predetermined objective. Akin to planning are budgeting and scheduling. Budgeting defines the future acts in terms of cost. Scheduling places them in a time frame. Both are necessary for the follow-up to planning: control.

If you review road maps and select the highways for a cross-country drive you are planning—if you determine how far you will travel each day so that you can reserve a motel room in advance—you are scheduling. If you set a limit for the money you will spend daily for food, accommodations, and gas, you are budgeting. The planning does you little good unless you check every now and then to see what road you are on and how far you have proceeded. Also you must examine the menu prices to see which entrées are permissible. That is the control phase.

A business is planned in the same way. You plan for those things that are important to you. If you want to assure yourself of profits, you make a profit plan. If you want individual products to stand on their own, you make product plans. If you want effective departments, you make departmental operating plans. And then there are cash plans, program plans, research and development plans, and investment plans. Everything a business does can be planned. Unfortunately, there must be a little time left in the day to make and to sell, so planning must be put in its proper niche in the hierarchy of business demands.

Is planning necessary?

Like that extra heartbeat when an attractive person walks by, planning may not be necessary but it happens anyway. Everyone does some planning, in the mind if not on paper. All things that are important should be planned carefully. Activities that are not important and cost little should not be planned. Predetermining which is which is time management, a form of planning.

The most valuable plan for a business is its marketing plan, because selling is the most important thing a company can do and is apt to be the most difficult. Therefore, it needs the most thought.

Next in value is the operating plan, because that is what turns new orders into profit. Most companies ought to have both a marketing plan and an operational plan, because selling and making is what they do. The plans are more effective when they are written down and thoroughly discussed with all key personnel.

The operating plan

An operating plan is a true control document, designed to establish a specific relationship between the amount of money a company spends and the level of its productivity. The numbers that are set down are those that are to be followed by all employees. An operating plan can be effective for that period of time for which the new orders or the work backlog can be predicted reliably. The sales figures in the operating plan are not forecasts, they are budgets.

It starts with a work-input forecast

The only unknown in an operating plan is the level of new orders (bookings) that the company will receive. If the company works on a quick turnaround basis it will have a low backlog, and therefore the forecast of bookings will determine the operating level of the company as a whole.

The operating plan is good only so long as the predicted input level can be maintained.

For most companies the predicted input level depends upon a booking forecast that is reliable for at least three months into the future.

The marketing plan

Because a predictable level of new orders is so important, companies that want to do a better job of selling and of predicting create a marketing plan. Unlike the operating plan, a marketing plan is based on conjecture, on value judgment, and on intuition. The booking figures are not budgets, they are quotas. A quota is a number set as a goal for a salesman or a group of salesmen.

The marketing plan starts with an evaluation of the market and then selects the portion in which the company is most interested. A marketing plan envelops everyone in the company because the service provided must match the market segment selected. It should explain what is being sold and the benefits to the customers (see chapter 5), and, if possible, it should state exactly which customers are to be sought. It should apportion territories or customers among the salesmen and formulate quotas based on past history, salesman commitments, and other factors that can be justified.

A marketing plan starts off as a premise, so it must be improved to the level of a pseudo-science, and this is done by keeping information and correlating sales with marketing efforts. When it looks like something really works the word is passed.

Can a retail store have a marketing plan? Of course. Start off with the type of neighborhood being served. List the characteristics of the people in the neighborhood. See whether there is a way to match the clerk's actions and the company's decor to those traits. Should price signs be displayed? Should help be volunteered? Should goods be displayed on counters, or on racks? What kind of goods are most likely to be sold? These things should be discussed, and decisions should be made and written down. Comments should be noted. Customers questioned and results recorded. Trends reviewed for any possible implications.

The profit plan

With a reliable new order forecast a company can construct a valid profit plan, which is the major portion of the operating plan. The profit plan breaks down costs of sales and expenses. In manufacturing companies the cost of sales is further broken down into direct labor, direct material, purchased parts, subcontracts, and manufacturing overhead expenses.

The cost of sales can be related to different products as well. See figure 4-1 for an example of a profit plan.

General expenses can be broken out by department and be used as departmental budgets. See figure 4-2, which is an indirect expense budget derived from the profit plan shown in figure 4-1.

Cash planning

Another extremely valuable planning tool is the cash-flow forecast. Receipts and expenditure forecasts are revised whenever sales levels change. Changes in sales, either upward or downward, usually mean that cash variations are coming, too. Not necessarily in the same direction. Selling your current inventory and not buying additional products, based on a projected drop in sales, may result in extra cash. The appendix gives an example of a cash-flow forecast.

When it appears that your company may be running low on cash, there are a number of steps you can take to alleviate the problem:

- Push your customers to pay their bills faster.
- Pay your bills a little slower.
- Borrow.
- Reduce inventories.
- Cut expenses.

- Put off any capital improvements.
- Raise prices.

Follow-up

Planning without follow-up is a waste. If goals and budgets have been set, people must be rewarded or chastised for meeting or failing to meet their objectives. The reward may be a pat on the back or a "Well done." The punishment may be having to explain the failure. Reviewing budget performance is the task of the chief executive, perhaps with the assistance of the financial officer.

The customary way of identifying expenses against budgets is through the use of charge numbers. Every purchase order lists a charge against an expense account or a program. Similarly, employees fill out their time cards showing the hours worked on various tasks. The expenses are accumulated periodically, by hand or by computer, and compared with the original budget.

The business plan

A business plan is a "long-range" plan that is very much in vogue among investing groups. It is primarily a statement of objectives and a logical approach toward achieving them, and this portion is very helpful. It probably goes too far in quantifying, however. At best, a business plan is tentative, strategic in scope, and subjected to uncontrollable outside influences. Its value is in clarifying the thinking of management and providing a common goal. It is also demanded by potential investors.

The unfortunate aspect of most business plans is that they are comprised of many detailed figures that are always backed into. Once the company determines the kind of performance the potential investors want, the sales and earnings figures are manipulated to fit that condition. I have never seen it done any other way! (See chapter 6 for more information about preparing a business plan.)

SCHEDULING

Planning must be time-related. Scheduling is setting the future events into a time-controlled framework. The budget figures that control costs are not independent of time. If a company has a backlog of undelivered orders equal to $200,000 and the cost of sales is 70 percent, or $140,000, how quickly must the company deliver those goods if its monthly expenses are $15,000?

Because the expenses must be paid out of the $60,000 "gross margin," the company would exactly break even in four months. It would show a $15,000 profit if the orders were delivered in three months and a $15,000 loss if delivery took five.

Scheduling is the tool you use to get an order out in three months if you want it out in that time. There are different ways to schedule, and the simplest method that will get the job done is the one to use.

Bar chart

Figure 4-3 is an example of a bar chart. It is the simplest of all scheduling techniques. Each bar represents a task. The horizontal base denotes time, so the length of the bar is the estimated time span of the task. You can tell instantly when the task is supposed to be started and when it is supposed to be completed. If you draw a vertical line at any day, everything to the left will have been accomplished if you are on schedule. If you shade in the bars to denote completion, the darkened areas should always reach the current date line.

Bar charts were the only form of scheduling for many years. They can be made to work on the smallest or the largest jobs, are extremely easy to prepare, and can be read by anyone. They do not show interdependence of tasks, however. As a result it is difficult to distinguish between critical completion dates and less significant ones.

CPM and PERT

When tasks are complicated it may be necessary to account for their interrelationships. CPM (critical path monitoring)

Figure 4-1/XYZ Manufacturing Company Profit Plan, Year 197- (in thousands of dollars)

	Jan	Feb	Mar	Apr	May	Jun	3rd Qtr	4th Qtr	Year
New Orders									
Product A	20.0	20.0	20.0	20.0	20.0	25.0	75.0	80.0	280.0
Product B	20.0	20.0	25.0	30.0	30.0	30.0	105.0	120.0	380.0
Total	40.0	40.0	45.0	50.0	50.0	55.0	180.0	200.0	660.0
Net Sales									
Product A	20.0	20.0	20.0	20.0	20.0	20.0	75.0	75.0	270.0
Product B	20.0	20.0	20.0	25.0	25.0	30.0	95.0	105.0	340.0
Total	40.0	40.0	40.0	45.0	45.0	50.0	170.0	180.0	610.0
Cost of Sales:									
Product A									
Material	4.0	4.0	4.0	4.0	3.8	3.8	14.0	14.0	51.6
Direct labor	6.0	6.0	5.8	5.8	5.8	5.7	21.0	20.0	76.1
Product B									
Material	5.0	5.0	5.0	6.0	6.0	7.0	22.0	24.0	80.0
Direct labor	4.0	4.0	4.0	4.8	4.8	5.5	17.0	18.5	62.6
Indirect mfg. costs	12.0	12.0	12.0	12.2	12.2	12.4	39.1	43.8	155.7
Total	31.0	31.0	30.8	32.8	32.6	34.4	113.1	120.3	426.0
Gross margin	9.0	9.0	9.2	12.2	12.4	15.6	56.9	59.7	184.0
Percent gross margin	22.5	22.5	23.0	27.1	27.6	31.2	33.5	33.2	30.2%
General adm. expenses	7.0	8.0	9.0	9.0	7.0	7.6	26.0	26.2	99.8
Total costs	38.0	39.0	39.8	41.8	39.6	42.0	139.1	146.5	525.8
Pretax profits	2.0	1.0	0.2	3.2	5.4	8.0	30.9	33.5	84.2
Percent-pretax profits	5.0	2.5	0.5	7.1	12.0	16.0	18.2	18.6	13.8%

Note: Product A is a mature product with minimal growth, and the plan's objective is to reduce manufacturing costs. Product B is a growth product, and the plan is to increase sales.

Figure 4-2/XYZ Manufacturing Company/Expense Budget

	Jan	Feb	Mar	Apr	May	Jun	3rd Qtr	4th Qtr
MANUFACTURING INDIRECT								
Salaries and wages:								
Engineer	$1,500	$1,500	$1,500	$1,500	$1,500	$1,500	$4,500	$5,000
Buyer	1,000	1,000	1,000	1,000	1,000	1,000	3,000	3,300
Foreman	1,000	1,000	1,000	1,000	1,000	1,000	3,000	3,300
Planner/shipper	800	800	800	800	800	800	2,400	4,800
Payroll-related costs*	2,800	2,800	2,800	2,800	2,800	3,000	10,200	11,000
Rent	1,800	1,800	1,800	1,800	1,800	1,800	5,400	5,400
Utilities	600	600	600	600	600	600	1,800	1,800
Factory supplies	500	500	500	600	600	600	2,000	2,000
Tools	500	500	500	600	600	600	1,900	2,000
Equipment rental	300	300	300	300	300	600	1,200	1,800
Depreciation	500	500	500	500	500	600	1,500	1,500
Freight	300	300	300	300	300	300	1,000	1,000
Misc.	400	400	400	400	400	400	1,200	1,200
Total	$12,000	12,000	12,000	12,200	12,200	12,400	39,100	43,800
GENERAL EXPENSES								
Executive & sales salaries	3,800	3,800	3,800	3,800	3,800	4,000	12,000	12,000
Secretary	600	600	600	600	600	700	2,100	2,100
Payroll-related costs	600	600	600	600	600	700	2,100	2,100
Rent	200	200	200	200	200	200	600	600
Telephone and telegraph	400	400	400	400	400	400	1,200	1,200
Postage	100	100	100	100	100	100	300	300
Office supplies	200	200	200	200	200	200	600	600
Promotion & advertising	300	300	300	300	300	500	1,500	1,500
Travel and auto expense	400	400	400	400	400	400	1,200	1,200
Insurance	200	200	200	200	200	200	600	600
Legal and accounting	-	1,000	1,000	-	-	-	1,000	1,000
Local and state taxes	-	-	1,000	2,000	-	-	2,000	2,000
Misc.	200	200	200	200	200	200	800	1,000
Total	$7,000	8,000	9,000	9,000	7,000	7,600	26,000	26,200

*Payroll-related costs include company-paid insurance and taxes on direct and indirect personnel. Rent is allocated to factory and general by floor space occupancy.

and PERT (program evaluation and review technique) have been structured to do that. The techniques are quite similar but PERT is the more complex. When using PERT the estimator must provide for each "activity," three time spans: the most optimistic, the most pessimistic, and the one with the greatest probability.

Figure 4-4 shows a CPM chart with three paths. The top path is the critical path because it takes the longest time to complete. Any activity that is not completed on time will extend the overall schedule. There is slack time along the two lower paths. Activities there can fall somewhat behind schedule and not extend the overall schedule. The attention of the company management is therefore given to the critical path. It is a method of establishing priorities.

Large companies use a computer to prepare and to track the PERT and CPM charts, but this is not necessary. A hand-drawn chart will do very well.

Advantages and disadvantages of CPM and PERT

Scheduling systems are no better than the use made of them. In a small company, CPM and PERT may not be monitored because of the complexity of doing so. It is much better to have a simple bar chart that is monitored than stacks of PERT computer print-outs lying on someone's desk, unread.

The greatest advantage of CPM or PERT is the thought process required in its preparation. The act of defining relationships between tasks uncovers many sticky problems that otherwise would go undetected. CPM or PERT makes the planner think the job through in great detail.

In addition, CPM or PERT does establish scheduling priorities for the company that cannot afford to expedite every job in the house.

Details of the preparation of a CPM chart

Circles denote events. An event is a milestone. No time is required for milestones. They happen as a result of activities that are represented by the lines connecting the events.

Examples of events are:

Figure 4-3/Schedule Graph

Schedule: Main Valve
Program #2446

Customer: LY Water District
Delivery Required: Sept. 15

	APRIL	MAY	JUNE	JULY	AUGUST	SEPT.

Contract received

Design calculations

Casting drawings
Machined parts dwgs.

Procure casting
Other purchasing

Machine shop tasks

Welding

Assemble and test

Deliver

Dateline—July 1

Figure 4-4/Critical Path Diagram

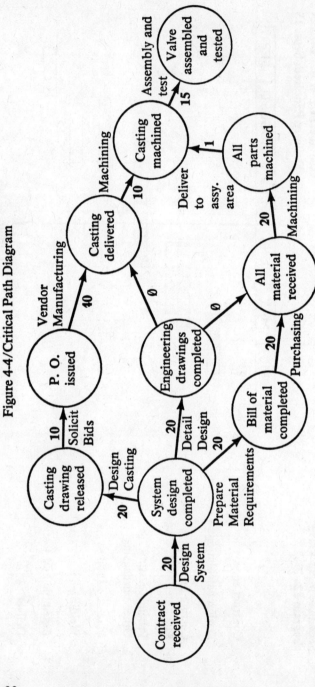

The top path is critical because it takes the most time to complete.
Minimum completion time= 20+20+10+40+10+15= 115 working days.

- Purchased parts are on dock.
- A subassembly is started.
- A test is completed.
- A system is sold off.

Examples of activities are:

- Design
- Fabrication
- Preparation of purchase orders

In many cases there is no need to define the activity, because the events bounding it make its meaning apparent. If two circles are *assembly started* and *assembly completed,* there is no need to explain that the activity is "assemble."

Manpower loading

Any scheduling technique can be combined with a man-hour estimate, and a manpower loading chart can be drawn up. Such a chart can be a valuable tool in anticipating hiring needs and in leveling work loads. Figure 4-5 shows three simple bar charts for a machine shop, with the man-hour estimates for each task in the three jobs. Figure 4-6 shows how the bar chart is used to give the manpower loading for the welding department. Each square represents one man-day. The number of man-days is determined by dividing the estimated man-hours by eight. This number is further divided by the number of days shown on the bar chart to give the average number of man-days per day for the task. The man-days are superimposed on the chart. Figure 4-6 shows an unusual peak of manpower. Rather than hire extra men for a short period, the shop operator should stretch out one of the tasks.

The example shown eliminates weekends from the monthly calendar. It makes drawing up the chart easier. If the manpower loading were prepared in man-weeks or man-months, eliminating nonworking days would not be necessary. Many factories work on an M-Day schedule that consecutively numbers the working days in the year eliminating weekends and holidays.

Scheduling by computer

There are scheduling and manpower-loading programs available for all the personal computers. These programs are good because they take CPM-type chart inputs and convert the information to a bar chart display. The bar chart is much easier to follow, particularly if there are many complex inter-related activities. Nevertheless, many companies with ample computer power still use manually prepared CPM or PERT charts. The reason is that while bar charts are easy to follow they are hard to critique. Managers cannot spot missing activities by easy examination. This is a valid criticism. For complex programs it is best to prepare a CPM chart by hand and to review it thoroughly for errors and omissions. Once corrected it can be entered into the computer for day-by-day follow-up. Periodically the hand chart can be updated in color providing an easy-to-understand overview.

INPUTS

People are the greatest obstacle to effective planning. They are usually reluctant to go out on the limb with estimates for which they may be held to account. Moreover, planning takes time away from work and is often seen as a waste. There are many theories about planning and how to handle the task of planning, but only one works: persistent nagging.

You must want to institute planning so much that you won't let up. When your employees finally understand that you are going to have your way, they will acquiesce.

Do not make the error of doing your employee's planning job for him. It will not work. First of all you are sure to overlook something, but even more important, there is no commitment. The person who makes the estimate is the only person who can logically be held responsible for it.

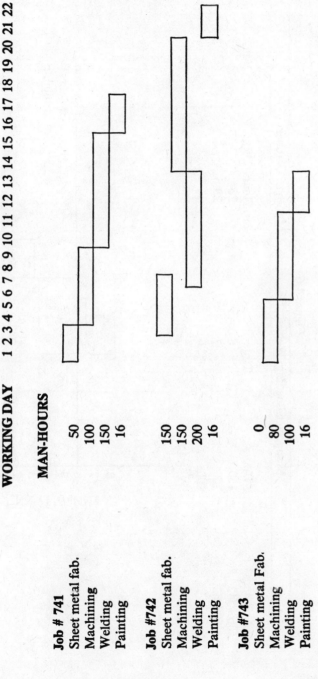

Figure 4-5/Machine Shop Schedule/Month of October

35

Figure 4-6

Manpower Loading/Welding Department/Month of October

	Man-Hours	Time Span	Man-Hours/Day	Equiv. Men
Job #741	150	6 days	25	3.1
Job #742	200	7	28.6	3.6
Job #743	100	6	16.6	2.1

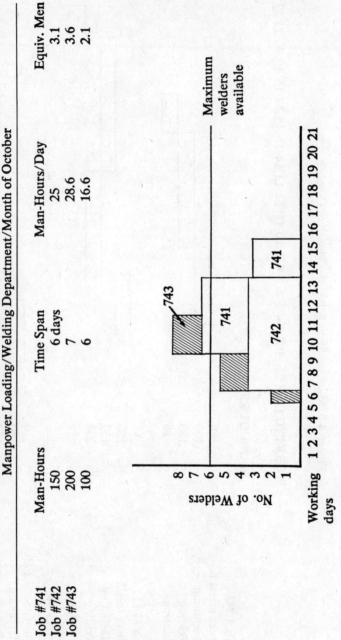

Make no mistake about it—of all business activities the planning activity creates the greatest conflict of wills between manager and employee. If you want good planning you cannot falter.

Planning sessions

One way to get your people to plan is to isolate them from every other business function. Take them out of the store into a hotel room or hold meetings out of town on a weekend.

Have everybody participate

Get as many people into the act as possible. Make them justify their estimates to their cohorts. Do not pay attention to departmental lines or individual status. Let anyone play the devil's advocate. Your employees know more about one another's frailties than you do. If they let their hair down you may get a surprisingly good session.

Do not be an active participant yourself

If you do not like the results of the planning session, wait until later to change it. Once you start expressing your opinion many of your employees will echo it. You will get the results you want but they may be all wrong, and you will come to wonder how a plan so well thought out could be such a dud. You are there to see they do the job, not to do it for them.

If a little is good, will a lot be better?

Planning can be overdone. Some companies demand so much planning that few hours are left to do real work. This may be a sign of insecurity on the part of management. It may want to be in a position to redirect action before it occurs. Results of such overplanning are usually bad. Employees resent spending so much time to prove they know what they are doing and having so little left to do what they feel is necessary. Overplanning destroys the planners' faith in management. It costs money, and it uses up valuable time.

Companies with government contracts get an overdose of such nonsense. The government may have more people reviewing plans than the company has working on the contract.

These government planning and administrative activities were put into effect over the years to compensate for contractor mismanagement and technical shortcomings. They were intended to reduce the cycle time of new systems from concept to deployment and also to reduce expenses. They did neither.

5
HOW GOOD
IS YOUR PRODUCT?

Business is the selling of a service of commercial value. That service is your "product." The product may be *tangible,* like hardware, or *intangible,* like financial advice. Whether you can hold your service in your hand or not, it is still a product. But be careful—your true product may be something other than the item you hand over the counter.

How important is product?

Your product is your reason for being in business. If it is the right one, your business may survive everything you do to destroy it.

Ampex survived a continuous sequence of inept management teams because of the quality and performance of its recording equipment.

Howard Hughes tried three times to pull his Hughes Aircraft Company away from electronic systems and back into the business he loved, aircraft. He failed because the Air Force kept giving the company orders for its excellent fire control systems.

What is your product?

If you own a jewelry store you may think you sell gems in lovely settings, but your product is more likely to be trust or prestige. After all, jewelry can always be obtained for a lower price at a discount house.

If you sell Ford automobiles your product is daily transportation, but if you sell Rolls Royces your product is prestige. The two cars do not fill the same need, and as a consequence their competition differs. Ford competes with Chevrolet, with the public transportation system, and with the repair shop that can restore seven-year-old Volkswagens. Rolls competes with sable coats, diamond brooches, and Chris-Craft cruisers.

The Mercedes may or may not compete against the Rolls. A car like the Mercedes or the Porsche or the 300Z is more likely to be an item of self-indulgence. You know that you do not need it and you may even feel a little diffident about owning one, but you want it anyway. It is an adult toy of the most expensive kind and competes against other performance cars but not necessarily against other toys. Most adults have only one or two types of toys they like to play with and are not easily switched to others.

Your product is defined not from the seller's viewpoint but from the buyer's. Defined by the need it fills, not the thing it is.

If you own a Kentucky Fried Chicken franchise your product is not chicken but convenience. Your competitor is the neighborhood supermarket and its frozen food counter.

Conversely, if you run a dinner house your product is entertainment. Your competitors are not the hash-joint down the street but the movie theatre, the concert hall, and the bowling alley. You are competing for your customer's night out. That is why you must have pleasant service and surroundings to go with your good food.

A product is a service that fills a need. Before there is a cure there must first be a disease.

The idea of carrying trailers on railcars, piggyback, was thought of in the early 1940s. It was used in some business schools as an example of a cure for which there was no known disease. In the mid-1950s, piggybacking caught on. Why? Because of increased highway traffic and higher road taxes on trucks.

Remember the guy who dove off the board only to notice that the pool was empty? He decided to go back! Well, his decision was right but his timing was lousy. Product timing can work the same way.

What is a good product?

A good product is one you can sell. The key word is *you*.

Suppose you were able to design a high-performance, low-cost automobile. Do you think you could make a business selling automobiles that you designed? Not a chance. Yet your car might be an instant success in General Motors' line. The difference? Organization. General Motors' dealer organization is what sells cars (and gives the buyer confidence that he can get the service he needs.)

Suppose you had a unique copier that could outperform its Xerox equivalent at a lower cost. That ought to be easy to sell, right? No easier than that car. If you had enough time and tens of millions of dollars you might eventually cut out a small piece of the market. Public prejudices would have to be overcome. The user has been conditioned to think of Xerox as the standard, and many companies have been burned by low-cost competitors claiming to have a superior product but who were unable to provide maintenance.

The more innovative your product, the tougher it will be to sell, the longer selling it will take, and the more it will cost. Nobody will beat a path to your door. It does not work that way anymore, if it ever did. People must be educated and convinced before they will accept new ideas or new products, unless "new" just means "better." Like NEW BOLD or NEW TIDE or NEW HEAD AND SHOULDERS, which means the same old product with a new ingredient. That, they buy.

David Ogilvy, the advertising genius, said that NEW is the second most powerful word in advertising (the first is FREE), but he did not mean NEW (radically different), he meant NEW (slightly modified).

Another obstacle is a market which is already dominated by a large company like IBM or a group of companies like the big three in automobiles. Since then, the Japanese car makers have successfully cut a major niche and the Germans have lopped off most of the very profitable top end. Individuals have had little success—DeLorean being a prime example.

The car makers became vulnerable to the Japanese because they believed in their invulnerability and ignored the consumer. They made a remarkable recovery once they had to meet the customers' needs. It is best to avoid confrontations with General Motors, General Electric, Xerox, and IBM because you won't have a government behind you.

On the other hand, it is possible to compete against large companies when they are not dominant. New food products are introduced successfully every day in spite of the existence of General Food and General Mills. It is not the size of the competitor which is important but the prejudice of the marketplace. IBM took over the personal computer business almost immediately after introducing the PC. When AT&T, a larger company with a better product, entered the field, it made very little impact.

Big companies innovate all the time. Why are they different?

Big companies can finance the pioneering task and the education that must accompany a new concept. It takes a lot, particularly if the product is not readily acceptable. Can you imagine a small company promoting the 45-rpm record player the way RCA did? They virtually gave it away to make a market for the records.

RCA tried that trick again with the video disc. This time it was a disaster. RCA wrote off a half billion bucks and went on to the next game. Do you want to take a risk like that?

Big companies generally pay for development and promotion out of current revenues. Their costs are expensed. As long as their current products are selling well they can afford this cost. One big winner pays for many losers.

A small company invests capital, and if there is not enough the product may fail a month away from success.

How do you know what products to sell?

There is no substitute for knowing your business and your customers' needs. You must be able to recognize when small variations will fill a need. Small variations do not equate with small sales but they do mean lower risk. Look for those small things.

There are many suppliers of *modems,* a device that permits digital data to be transmitted over telephone lines. One supplier noted that users were always arguing with the telephone company regarding service. When the modem did not work, the telephone company would disclaim responsibility. It is the modem, not the line, the company would say. The small manufacturer took advantage of this situation by building into his modems a test device that showed whether the signal failure was caused by the equipment, or by the telephone line. It was simple enough for any employee to understand. This idea resulted in many new sales. It was a small addition that filled a large need.

Reaching the customer

A small company cannot afford the selling costs of reaching consumers on a nationwide basis. It must sell on a limited, local basis or use an independent middleman organization like a broker or a distributor or a manufacturers' representative (sales rep).

If you are thinking of introducing a new product, make certain that there are groups who will accept your product and sell it on your behalf. Trade journals will tell you who they are. Talk to them. Solicit their advice. See whether they are enthusiastic. You will find that people in independent sales organizations are cooperative and helpful. They know the customer, so listen to what they have to say.

Warning: *Sales reps have rules about the things they sell. A single product is rarely enough. They want complete lines. If you have designed an ornamental hubcap you must be able to fit all wheel sizes.*

Many reps will not handle items with low sales prices, particularly if they are types of articles that are sold in small quantities. It is a matter of arithmetic. A sales call for industrial products costs anywhere from $50 to $200. The salesman must earn that much or more in commissions for every call.

He cannot, for example, afford to sell a $200 item on a call that takes three hours to demonstrate the device, unless multiple orders are possible.

Custom services

Your company may be built around a capability of providing custom services rather than standard services. Depending upon the industry you are in you may be called a custom builder, a specialty house, a made-to-order tailor, or a job-shop. If so, you sell your capability. It takes a long time to make a custom sale because the configuration must be defined and the customer convinced that you can do the job. You or your engineer or your designer will be the most effective salesmen. Reps will not be willing to spend the time necessary because it takes too long to earn commissions. You will not be able to contact many potential buyers, so you must concentrate on the best ones. In most cases companies making custom products do so for very few accounts. Ten customers usually will provide over 80 percent of the business. The success of the business will be determined by the quality of the customers. Winners go where the money is.

SELECTING YOUR NEW PRODUCT

Think it through

Before you embark on that new product adventure, think it through from start to final sale. Most important, picture how it will reach the ultimate customer. You would not open a hamburger stand on a rarely traveled country road, but a first-class dinner house might make it there.

Before point-of-sales terminals became commonplace, a number of small companies were in the business of making them. They all failed because they could not reach the customer to explain how to use their systems. They thought potential users would immediately recognize the merits, but they were wrong. Big companies like TRW with big sales forces dominate the business now.

Litton Industries has a successful microwave oven operation. Did you know that it once had an industrial microwave oven division that failed miserably? It failed to prove to industrial users that microwave cooking had any advantage. It did not think its product through to the end-user. Speed of cooking, which was a convenience to the harried housewife, was much less important than cost and consistency to food processors.

Creativity

Creativity, like innovation, should match the means. Fields that depend on creativity, such as theatrical producing, publishing, and recording, are dangerous for the small businessman, who because of capital limitations must start off with winners. At the same time, these high-risk fields are the ones that provide large returns.

Many mundane products require creative talent. Market acceptance may depend on an aesthetic quality like style or appearance rather than on functional performance. Exceptional styling may bring premium prices. If the product you produce can benefit from eye appeal, have it styled by a professional.

During the height of the mobile home boom in 1969 a diversified conglomerate bought a very successful mobile home manufacturer for what appeared to be a bargain price. The president of the selling company took his share of the proceeds and left for greener pastures. That did not worry the buyer because it saw no magic in making mobile homes. A new president was found. He had been a promoter of Florida real estate and obviously was a man who could sell homes. Yet, in a year the company's sales dropped to half. The conglomerate had not taken the former president's personal activities into account. He was the one who had designed all the interiors. It was their appeal that had sold the product. When he left he took with him the company's most important asset, his own talent.

Other kinds of talent

There is a talent for reading the marketplace, predicting accurately what people will buy. People who do this understand that products are need-filling things, and never lose the perspective of the user.

Diane Von Furstenburg, a princess and member of the jet set, made an overnight success in the clothing business by acting on her belief that women would still buy attractive dresses in an era when pantsuits were all the rage.

A new company made a successful entry into the leather goods business by guessing that status-conscious businessmen would buy extremely high-priced attaché cases.

Calvin Klein dreamed up the high-fashion blue jean and carved a niche that Levi Strauss had not even thought about.

Wang took a mundane computer design and tailored it to the business office.

Nolan Bushnell made the computer small enough to be a kid's toy.

The two Steves made their computer just a little larger and made it an adult's toy. In so doing, they created a whole new segment of the computer industry with far-reaching business implications. The kids' toy didn't do nearly so well.

It is interesting to reflect that the Jobs and the Wozniacs and the Wangs and the Perots and the Bushnells and others became multimillionaires carving out small pieces of the computer market while John Mauchly and Pres Eckert who really started the whole industry ended up working for Sperry Corp.

Shortening the odds

Although product success cannot be assured, the odds against failure can be improved. This means giving up the long shot, the hoola hoop and the home permanent. It means sticking with concepts that have been proved and adding that little extra.

Television producers do this all the time, by copying successful formulas. It may detract from the artistic quality of the programming but it keeps a network from bombing out on a grand scale. On the whole, viewers do not watch drastically different shows. The TV producer puts survival ahead of innovation. So should you.

The "ideal" product for a small business

Here are the characteristics of the product most likely to survive:

- It is similar to other products that people buy in large quantities. (It is easily recognizable and the market is relatively large.)

- It has all of the features of competitive products and performs as well or better in all respects. (It is not necessary to explain away any deficiencies.)

- It has at least one significant advantage over its competition, such as better appearance, more functions, superior performance, or lower price. (There is a strong selling point.)

- There is no dominant supplier in the marketplace. (It is not necessary to overcome customer prejudices.)

Product life

No product lasts forever. They are all replaced by better ideas growing out of new technologies or are abandoned as needs change. Be prepared to upgrade your product to keep it competitive and to drop it when it is no longer capable of carrying its load. Do not keep products to satisfy personal ego. If you make a mistake, admit it and try again. Do not allow your employees to make product life a personal issue. No one likes to see his brain-child die, but there is a time when this must come.

Make product appraisal a continual practice

Never take your product for granted. Know it. Look at it frequently. Try it out, if you can. Get all the inputs possible. From your friends, customes, salesmen, end-users. Forget the praise. Listen to the criticisms, the hedged answers, and the unspoken words. Find out whether they are valid. Recognize your weaknesses before your competitors can.

Study your competitor. Keep track of his ideas. Try to divine where he is heading. You may want to cut him off at the pass. You can never learn enough about your product or your competitor, so keep at it.

Do not underestimate your competitors

Your competitor needs his business as much as you need yours. He wants to succeed just as much as you do. He may be as smart as you. Just hope he makes the mistake of under-estimating you, but do not return that favor.

There are three common ways of underestimating your competitors:

- Thinking you see a market no one else sees.

- Basing your plans on what competitors are doing now.

- Thinking you have them hopelessly outmaneuvered.

The thermosetting plastics industry and the semiconductor industry are excellent examples of enticing new markets that attracted capital assets and capacity at a rate that far out-paced the rapid rate of market growth. Each producer thought that it could get a stranglehold on the new, virgin territory. The result was rapid development and price competition beyond anyone's wildest expectations.

Bowmar is an example of a company that based its plans on what its competitors were doing rather than on what the competitors would do. This company took a strong lead in the hand-held calculator business but was destroyed by the influx of price-cutters. Its major competition came from the companies that made large-scale integrated circuits, the heart of the calculator.

Westinghouse entered the semiconductor business a number of years ago, believing it had a technological edge on its competition in a lower-cost process. It came out with a low-priced line of semiconductors, expecting to pick up a lion's share of the market. Whether edge was real or fancied, their competitors more than met the new prices and quickly cut the newcomer off from the market. Westinghouse withdrew, having benefited no one but the customer.

One thing to remember: *Your competitors will always react to attacks on their business. Their reaction may be more violent than you anticipate. They may also be illogical. But react they will, so be ready.*

Product protection

You should protect your product ideas from appropriation by others as best you can but without making a fetish of it. As a rule your competitors will have a low regard for any ideas that are not their own, but there is no point in taking chances.

If your product is unique, it may be patentable. Whether you apply for a patent should depend upon the long-range potential of the product and your ability to police and enforce the patent.

Quite often it is better to keep your product secret than it is to patent it. Unfortunately, almost any product can be *reverse engineered*. That is, examined and dissected by knowledgable persons to determine its working secrets. Reverse engineering is legal, provided the product has not been obtained under false pretenses. Anyone has the right to buy a product, reverse engineer it, and sell a duplicate unless the product is patented. Although it is hard to keep the makeup of devices secret, it is possible to keep formulas and process techniques out of circulation.

You can protect proprietory ideas from disclosure by treating them as secrets and by requiring employees and other parties to sign nondisclosure agreements. This is a precaution that costs little and may save much. Your attorney can draft an agreement for you, but it is easier and less expensive to get from the personnel office of a nearby large corporation a sample that you can copy. Have each of your employees sign one of these agreement forms before starting work or when receiving a raise.

The government will steal your ideas

All government development contracts and many of the supply contracts contain a "Rights in Data" clause. This should really be entitled "No Rights in Data." Little by little, in spite of a fierce holding action by the more innovative companies, the government is making it impossible for anyone to keep proprietary rights to his ideas or his processes. At the present time you can forestall use of your ideas for a few years, but this may not continue. The bad part is that the right that the government takes is not for its exclusive use but for everyones' use, including your competition. The idea behind this robbery is that the government is entitled to competitively bid everything it buys.

This tendency of the government to take over the ideas of others is nothing new. It has gone on for fifty years or so. What is new now is that there are few ways to fight it if you want to sell to the government. There are a growing number of companies that have decided that they do not want to sell to United States agencies. Others have surrendered proprietary rights after long struggles.

That's the way it is. I don't look for the pendulum to swing back.

FRANCHISING

Franchising lets a small businessman use someone else's product idea for his own. What's more, the idea will have a history, so it can be evaluated.

Advantage of buying a franchise

The main advantage of a franchise is its immediate recognition. Wherever people go they recognize the golden arches of McDonald's and know exactly what kind of hamburger to expect. As Holiday Inn advertises, there are no surprises.

A franchise generally is a highly predictable investment. If the return suits your fancy and the type of work will hold your interest, a franchise can be a wise choice.

What you may not like about a franchise

The successful franchises are expensive. There will be a maximum limit on what you will earn with one location.

Franchisers are particular about your following their company rules. There is no allowance for trying out your own ideas. (They permit no innovations at all.) What's more, you are both an employee and a customer to the franchiser. You won't always know where his well-intentioned advice stops and his self-interest begins.

If you have a yen for your own business but do not have any ideas how to go about it, you should consider buying a franchise. Before you sign on the dotted line, though, be sure you investigate the franchiser thoroughly. Have your accountant check his financial condition, have an attorney check the contract, and you spend a good amount of time talking to other franchisees.

6

HOW TO RAISE MONEY

I was going to call this chapter "How To Raise Money When You Need It." Then I remembered that old bromide about banks. It is true. The hardest time to borrow money is when you need it.

If you were to review the causes for small business failures you might come to the same conclusion I did: many failures were foreordained. The business did not have enough capital going in. This is going to be a recurring theme. If there is one thing you should remember from chapter 6, it is to get enough to do the job.

Where does the money come from?

There are only three ways for you to get money for your business:

- Put it up yourself (out of your savings).

- Borrow it.

- Sell some of the company.

Ways number two and three can be combined into one transaction (such as by selling convertible debentures).

Watch the cash

If you have a viable company it will reach a point where it will generate cash. You must be able to predict when this will happen. The appendix has a section on cash-flow forecasts. Every business should maintain one, at least until the bank account starts building. Large companies keep cash-flow forecasts as standard management tools. What it will do for you is tell you how much you need to get over the hump.

What is a security?

Securities have come to be defined by the Securities Exchange Acts and the Securities Exchange Commission. A security turns out to be just about any piece of paper issued by a company in exchange for money, except short-term notes. Stocks of all types are securities. So are convertible debentures, warrants, bonds, etc. These are the things you will use to obtain long-term financing. The definition is important because state and federal laws governing the sale of securities are very extensive.

THE LEGALITIES OF STOCK SALES

The sale of securities through the mail and across state lines is regulated by the Securities and Exchange Act of 1933 and 1934 and by the Securities Exchange Commission established by the 1933 Act. Sale of securities within a state is governed by the laws of that state.

State laws vary, but as a practical matter there is only one kind of security transaction you, your associates, or your company can undertake unless you get competent legal guidance. That transaction is the *private placement*.

Before you solicit your neighbors or potential employees for money in exchange for stock, see your lawyer. You may be making a public offering forbidden by your state. You might even be violating federal laws if you used the mails.

Why all this nonsense? *Neither the federal government nor your state wants unregulated securities falling into the hands of unsophisticated buyers. Therefore, your company is allowed to raise money only from a few knowledgeable individuals or organizations who are willing to hold the securities for a long period of time.*

So the first thing you must learn is the definition of private placement.

Private Placement

The 1933 Act, Section 4(2) establishes as an exemption "Transactions by an issuer not involving any public offering." This definition is too vague to stand on its own, so the SEC had to formulate rules and make specific decisions. In June 1974 it released Rule 146, the so-called safe-harbor rule for private placements. If you sell stock without the guidance of a competent attorney be certain to follow Rule 146 without exception.

How to make a safe private placement

If you follow these guidelines you will be making a private placement that falls within the limits of Rule 146:

- There must be direct contact between the issuer and the prospective purchasers where those contemplating buying can ask questions about the business.

- The offeree must have access to all information which would normally be available in a full registration.

- Purchasers must be limited to thirty-five in any twelve-month period.

- There must be no scheme to avoid registration or to circumvent any law.

- All offerees must be financially knowledgeable and able to bear the risk of a loss.

- There must be no general solicitation or advertising. Limit the number of active offerees to thirty-five.

- Have a legend imposed on every stock certificate describing its limited disposition (see fig. 6–1).

- Have all purchasers sign an investment letter (see fig. 6–2).

- Issue only one stock certificate to each investor, regardless of the number of shares he has purchased.

- Prior to the purchase provide each offeree with an identical package composed of the following information:
  a. accurate, current financial statements;
  b. full description of securities offered;
  c. intended use of proceeds;
  d. relationship of issuer to offeree representative (if there is one);
  e. explanation of the investment nature of the transaction and the limitations on the rights of disposal of the security;
  f. disclosure of any ways in which security holders will be treated in an unlike manner.

The above should help you steer clear of any SEC problems but not of any state problems. A few states, such as California, New York, Texas, Illinois, have restrictions which will make the placement more complex. If you are making a private placement without benefit of a lawyer, write to your state corporate commissioner or department of corporations and get a copy of the state laws. Most of them are easy to understand.

FINANCING THE SMALL COMPANY

How much do you need?

You must start out with enough money to see you to the point where more cash comes in than goes out. You can figure out how much you will need and how long you will need it by making a cash-flow forecast.

Warning! *Never assume you can get a loan, unless you have a firm commitment. New entrepreneurs often believe that all they need is a large contract or a good backlog or sufficient security, and then any bank will rush to lend them money. Do not believe anything you hear. The only time a bank will lend you money is when it wants to lend it to you. Nobody can predict when that will be.*

The cash-flow forecast you make will be an invaluable aid in your money-raising chores.

Types of financing available

Although large public corporations seem to have an infinite number of schemes for raising money from the public and from institutions, privately held companies of modest means have only three:

- Sale of common stock.
- Secured loans.
- Long-term (secured or unsecured) with an equity "kicker" in the form of warrants or conversion rights.

These three must fall under the private placement exemption rules. You must look for well-off individuals and for companies that make investments as a business.

What a lender wants

Before you start shopping around for loans you ought to know what a lender wants for his money. Remember, lenders have little to gain from the loans they make, so they will be very conservative. Do not be misled by those cheerful television commercials about that friendly all-purpose bank and its smiling loan officer. An institution that makes its profits from the interest it collects will have to be convinced:

- That the borrower can repay the loan out of his normal business activities.

The following abbreviations, when used in the inscription on the face of this certificate, shall be construed as though they were written out in full according to applicable laws or regulations:

TEN COM —as tenants in common

TEN ENT —as tenants by the entireties

JT TEN —as joint tenants with right of survivorship and not as tenants in common

UNIF GIFT MIN ACT—

_____Custodian_____

(Cust)   (Minor)

under Uniform Gifts to Minors

Act_____

(State)

Additional abbreviations may also be used though not in the above list.

For Value Received,_____hereby sell, assign and transfer unto

PLEASE INSERT SOCIAL SECURITY OR OTHER
    IDENTIFYING NUMBER OF ASSIGNEE

_____

(Please print or typewrite name and address, including zip code, of assignee)

_____

_____

_____ Shares
of the capital stock represented by the within Certificate, and do hereby irrevocably constitute and appoint

_____ Attorney
to transfer the said stock on the books of the within named Corporation with full power of substitution in the premises.

Dated_____

NOTICE: THE SIGNATURE TO THIS ASSIGNMENT MUST CORRESPOND WITH THE NAME AS WRITTEN UPON THE FACE OF THE CERTIFICATE IN EVERY PARTICULAR, WITHOUT ALTERATION OR ENLARGEMENT OR ANY CHANGE WHATEVER.

"THE SHARES REPRESENTED BY THIS CERTIFICATE HAVE NOT BEEN REGISTERED UNDER THE SECURITIES ACT OF 1933 AND MAY NOT BE SOLD OR TRANSFERRED IN THE ABSENCE OF SUCH REGISTRATION OR AN EXEMPTION THEREFROM UNDER SAID ACT."

THIS SPACE MUST NOT BE COVERED IN ANY WAY

Figure 6-1/Stock Certificate Form (Back Side, Showing Legend)

XYZ CORPORATION
Address

Gentlemen:

This letter is furnished to you in connection with the sale to me of 1,000 shares (the "Shares") of Common Stock of the XYZ Corpora tion. In this connection I represent to you as follows:

1. I am aware that the offer and sale of the Shares to me has not been registered under the Securities Act of 1933 (the "Act") and tha the Shares must therefore be retained by me indefinitely and may not be resold by me except pursuant to an effective registration stateme under the Act or pursuant to an applicable exemption from such regis tion. I understand that you have no obligation to me to take any action which would result in the registration of the Shares or make exemption from such registration available to me.

2. I understand that the basis for the sale of the Shares to me wit registration under the act is the exemption for private placements. While I understand that I am neither an "issuer" nor a "dealer" I al understand that were I taking the Shares with a view to making a "distribution" (i.e., a public offering) of them, I might become an "underwriter" within the meaning of Section 4(1) and consequently the exemption from registration afforded by that Section (transactio by persons other than issuers, underwriters, and dealers) would not available to me. Accordingly, I represent to you that I am acquirin the Shares for investment and without a view to their distribution i whole or in part. I agree that any certificate evidencing any of th Shares may be endorsed with a legend indicating that the Shares have not been registered under the Act, have been acquired for investment and may not be resold absent registration under the Act unless an exemption from such registration is available in connection with a proposed resale. I agree that the Corporation may issue a "stop-transfer" order to the transfer agent in respect to these certificat

3. I have been offered access to all information concerning the Cor oration and have examined their latest financial returns. I am familiar with the business of the Corporation. The information I have examined is sufficient to evaluate the merits and risks of an investment in the Corporation.

4. I am financially able to make the investment represented by the Shares. In this connection I am able to hold the Shares indefinitel without materially affecting my financial condition and, were a comp loss in value of the Shares to occur, it would not materially affect financial condition.

5. The foregoing information has been provided to induce the XYZ Corporation to sell the Shares to me, knowing that they and their legal counsel will rely upon such information in determining whether the exemption provided by the Act is available with respect to the offer and sale of the Shares to me.

Very truly yours,

Figure 6-2/Sample Investment Letter

- That the loan is big enough to do the job. (There it is again.)

You will notice that no mention is made of collateral or net worth. That is because the lender is not in the business of foreclosing. Foreclosure proceedings reduce profits. Profits come from interest collected, nowhere else. Of course, the lender will insist on security anyway, because it prevents an occasional mistake from turning into a disaster, but it is not sufficient by itself to swing a loan.

So when you go for your loan, take along your cash-flow forecast and all the backup information like rental agreements and material costs and payroll expenses. It also helps if you bring résumés of key people.

Even if you pass all tests with flying colors, banks may still turn you down. Other factors are involved, such as the availability of credit, their loan load, the requirements of their regular customers, the rediscount rate, and the national economy. Don't go away mad. Get them to make you some sort of commitment, informal or not, as to the circumstances under which they will lend you money. Leave a copy of your cash-flow forecast with them. You may have cause to come back some day. They will be impressed if you have done what you predicted.

Your first loan is going to be the hardest. You and the other principals will have to pledge your own resources, too. The limited-liability feature of incorporation will not protect you from the banks. However, as time goes on and your company prospers, you may be able to squeeze out of any personal commitment, though you may have to go to a different bank to do it.

What an equity investor wants

People and organizations invest in small companies to make a killing. Unless you have a rich uncle or some benevolent angel who wants to help you get started, you had better be prepared to show your sophisticated offeree how he can make large capital gains by investing in your company. Talking about dividend potential will not raise a penny. In addition to showing the offeree how he can make those large gains, you must show him how he can get out. In other words, not only must his investment grow, it must be marketable. This usually requires plans for going public, but it may also envisage a sale to a large company in the future.

What constitutes a killing?

This is highly subjective and varies from time to time, but if you do not have specific knowledge of the potential investor's guidelines, start by showing him how he can increase his money tenfold in five or fewer years. Or show how the stock value will double every year for the next three or four years.

Am I joking? No, not a bit. People take big risks to make big gains. No matter how your business looks to you, if it has not been operating profitably for at least three years it is strictly blue sky to the investor. He needs big winners to compensate for the losers he knows he will have. Even if you could convince him the risk was small, you probably would not influence the price, although you would increase his enthusiasm.

How a venture capital company evaluates potential clients

Figure 6–3 shows the check-off sheet of a venture capital company that makes equity investments of $500,000 to $2,000,000 in relatively new businesses. This is a fairly typical list.

Be ready for the questions. Prepare a package that shows:

- An exciting new product or new concept in a growth market.

- Some protection against competition. A patent, a trade secret, special talent, or a process that will take years to duplicate.

- A capable management team and hopefully some prestigious scientists or artists or professionals.

- A comprehensive business plan.

I. COMPANY
  A. History: when founded, corporation formed, where, when.
  B. List divisions, subsidiaries, joint ventures, etc.
  C. How long have units been in business and part of the company.
  D. Present ownership distribution (list all shareholders).
  E. Professional services: legal counsel, CPA firm, commercial banks.

II. PRODUCT AND MARKET
  A. Describe products or services (include product brochures or descriptive literature).
  B. Describe percent of sales and income for each product line.
  C. Describe distribution channels.
  D. Describe the market (size, geographic, concentration).
  E. Major customers and suppliers.

III. FINANCIAL DATA
  A. Audited Income statements and Balance Sheets for past 5 years.
  B. Interim Financials, including most currrent balance sheet.
  C. Projection of company sales, profits and cash requirements for next 3 years.
  D. Balance Sheets Adjustments.
  E. Depreciation method—is it consistent with the past.
  F. How are inventories valued.
  G. Date of most recent tax audit.

IV. OPERATIONS
  A. List facilities.
  B. Capacity of present facility.
  C. R & D.
  D. Will management stay.

Minimum Information Required Before Ms
Can Act on a Potential Acquisition Situation

  A. Product Brochures or descriptive literature.
  B. Income Statements and Balance Sheets for past 3 years.
  C. Interim financials, including most current balance sheet.
  D. Projection of Sales, Earnings and Cash Requirements for next 3 years.

Figure 6-3/Information Requested for Screening
Potential Acquisition Candidates

- A five-year investment analysis showing growth in the book value and the earnings per share, and leading to a public offering.

You can see that the search for an equity investor usually requires a commitment to go public and to pay for the registration of your investor's stock. Otherwise the investor would be locked in with no way to sell his position. As a practical matter, when you do decide to go public, your underwriter will have a lot to say about how much stock your investors can sell in the offering.

One other thing that greatly influences venture capital companies: how much of your savings you have put into the company. If all the money going in is to be theirs, you can bet they will want most of the company if they do decide to invest. You will have to put *your* money where your mouth is if you want the best deal.

How to make an effective business plan

Because they are usually compiled for the benefit of outside investors, business plans must look good and have the ring of authenticity. A potential investor has probably seen hundreds of business plans, so he can tell a good one from a bad one.

Even though most business plans are contrived and the figures backed into, there is a difference between good ones and bad ones. The good ones have a foundation of facts and are consistent within themselves. The results are mathematically derived from a set of assumptions that have a logical origin. The plan must exhibit knowledge and must be presented in a way to make it appear conservative. The tone must be one of restraint.

The most important aspect of the business plan is the treatment it gives the company's markets and competition and the case it makes for increasing the company's share of those markets. The investor may discount the five-year forecast but is bound to be impressed with a thorough discussion of your market position. What is more, the work you do on preparing that portion will help you shape the company's goals. Do a good job of the business plan for your own benefit.

The business plan should include these sections:

- The product or service offered. Why it is unique. How it can be protected from competition.

- The market the product serves. Who, where, and how much. Where this information comes from. Past history, growth trends. How the company will reach this market.

- The competitors. Who, where, and how much. Percentage of market for each company. Trends. Weaknesses and strengths. How your comany fits in.

- A five-year new-order forecast with justification for the estimates. Show monthly for the first year, then quarterly. Name the customers if possible. Tie to published information; market growth, population, GNP, government budgets, whatever fits best. Break out by company products. Be as specific as possible.

- A five-year profit and loss forecast (proforma). Break out by product line. Detail cost of sales for each product. Elaborate on expenses. Give backup information.

- A five-year cash-flow forecast showing all new investment requirements.

- Proforma balance sheets for the coming five years.

- Capital equipment and new facility requirements.

- Personnel growth by department.

- New product development. Growth plans.

When you have completed this you will have an extensive document. Make sure your employees know about it, have contributed to it, and agree with it. Nothing is more embarrassing than to have the prospective investor keyed up over your plan and then run into one of your principal executives who blandly contradicts it. Of course it will not happen twice, but why let it happen at all?

The debt-equity investor

Institutions such as investment companies, venture capital companies, and special funds will almost assuredly want the best of both worlds. They will want interest on the funds they provide, a priority position over the stockholders in case of liquidation, and large capital gains if the company goes as projected. The fundseeker must show everything he would show to a lender and everything he would show to an equity investor, with one exception. It will not be necessary to show how the loan will be repaid, because the lender will be converting it to a common stock position at the appropriate time.

Loan agreements

Long-term equity type loans are accompanied by restrictive, even onerous, loan agreements. There may be provisions whereby the lender can assume control over your company in case of a default. This frequently happens, so be careful about what you sign. Do not be afraid to negotiate the terms and conditions. You will not lose a loan because you are a tough negotiator.

Know your lender

Lender-client relationships are tenuous even when things are going well. Each is wary of the other and is apt to misinterpret the most innocent statements. If the business turns sour there is often a falling out. The lender may conclude that the entrepreneur is unequal to the task and is unwilling to seek help. The businessman believes he is only a step or two from working out of his difficulties and feels the financial people are smothering him with requirements for detailed information and with obvious but unworkable advice.

As you might expect, both could be correct. There are plenty of short-sighted financiers, and a large number of entrepreneurs are poor managers.

Being open and above-board from the start may develop a relationship that will see you through the hard times. Unfortunately, it does not always work that way. Employees of financial institutions may use your own words to build a case against you.

Your best protection is a thorough checkout of the financiers before you sign a loan agreement. If they do not check out properly and you have to sign up anyway, try to develop a good friend within the organization, one who will stand up for you in their discussions and who will give you advance warning about adverse actions.

SOURCES OF CAPITAL

Short-term loans

The best place to borrow money is a commercial bank. It will give you the best service at the lowest cost. Obviously, then, it is the choosiest. A young company will not get a bank loan unless the principals have sufficient net worth and are willing to be guarantors. Even then, the bank may turn down the loan because it is close to its loan limit. Banks have to look after their regular customers first.

If you are fortunate enough to get a bank loan it will be one of two types: an open account, or a revolving account secured by accounts receivable and inventory.

An open line is an agreement by the bank to lend up to the line limit in 90- or 180-day notes. As you pay off one note you can take down another. It is also possible to renew notes. However, an open line of credit must be paid down to zero at least once a year. It is meant to supply a company's need for temporary funds of an emergency or cyclical nature. Such funds are not intended to provide the company's permanent working capital.

Revolving accounts are set up against a company's invoices and inventory. *Floors* are revolving accounts made against inventory only. The bank will lend up to a percentage of the face value of the company's invoices (usually 80 percent) and a percentage of the book value of the inventory (not the selling price). Inventory percentages vary greatly, depending on the type and the turnover. Receipts are deposited in a collateral account and are applied aganst the loan balance.

If an invoice is not collected within a prescribed period (usually 60 to 90 days), it is eliminated from the borrowing base. Likewise, special receivables such as those to government agencies and those on jobs that require surety bonds may be considered ineligible for a loan. They will still be part of the security, however.

With a revolving account a borrower pays higher interest but uses the money only so long as the invoice is outstanding, so actual interest costs may be lower than with a fixed-term note.

Compensating balances

Banks often make a company's minimum bank balance a condition of granting a line of credit. This allows them to increase their interest rates artificially by making you supply some of the money they will lend to you.

Commercial credit companies

There are a large number of commercial credit companies with highly ethical lending policies. These companies will make loans against accounts receivable and inventory much as the banks will, except that their rates are slightly higher and are usually quoted on a daily basis, like 1/25 percent per day. They will service viable companies who want to borrow more than the banks are willing to lend. Because they do not have to follow the state banking regulations or face bank examiners, they have more leeway to work with small companies than the banks. They will also help finance equipment purchases.

Factors

A factor is the most expensive of the lenders and provides very little except the service of making collections on behalf of the borrower. A factor charges a daily rate from the time he receives an invoice until the time he collects for that invoice. He may charge an extra day's interest on both ends of the transaction. Factor rates may run as high as 3 percent per month, but they may be your last source of additional financing.

Assigned receivables

Factors and credit companies require that invoices be *perfected,* that is, made payable to them. They will require that your customer be notified where and to whom to make payment. In some industries this is a stigma but in others it is the norm. Few companies assign their receivables, however, unless they have no choice.

Long-term loans

A new company must look to the Small Business Administration if it wants a long-term loan. The SBA will not make the loan directly unless the company cannot obtain a bank loan. The SBA will make it possible to get bank loans as high as $400,000 by guaranteeing 90 percent of the loan made by the bank.

SBA guaranteed loans are secured by all of the assets of the borrowing company and by the personal guarantee of one or more of the principals. The loan size may exceed the security, however.

Because liens against the accounts receivable and inventory preclude short-term borrowing, the SBA may release these in favor of a lender.

Taking out an SBA guaranteed loan will make it impossible to get any other long-term loan, because of the security position of the government. When your company qualifies for an insurance company loan it will have to borrow enough to pay off the SBA note.

Equity investment possibilities

Private individuals and local investment groups often make purchases of common stock in small companies. The most likely candidates are those who know you and believe in what you are doing. Sometimes a family-run venture capital fund will buy stock in a private company. If the product is exceptionally exciting, a venture capital fund might take a straight equity position. Chances are that it would hold out for a convertible debenture or note with warrants.

Venture capital and investment companies

There are a large number of venture capital companies, closed-end investment companies, and licensed small business investment companies (SBICs) that might be induced to make an equity type loan to your company. They would be particularly interested if you have been established a year or two and are profitable and growing. The economic climate will determine the deal that can be made. As previously stated, shop very carefully and check out the investor very thoroughly before proceeding. Talk to all of their clients if you can.

Many banks have associated small business investment companies. To find out, simply call the bank's main office and ask. The bank SBICs have a reasonably good client relationship, as compared with others.

Bank lending officers and the finance department managers of securities dealers are good sources for information regarding active venture capital sources.

Financial consultants, brokers, and finders

There are many people who will promise to raise money for your company but few who will deliver. Some will take money up front and give nothing in return. Others will agree to work for a percentage and then broadcast your needs to the world, hoping to hit a responsive receiver. On the other hand, there are a few who can work miracles for you and who are worth their fees. The task is to tell which is which. Again, you have to find and check with satisfied clients. There is no other reliable source of information.

Regarding fees; *Many brokers ask for payments regardless of results. If you elect to go with such a broker, pay him by the hour. It is unwise to agree to pay a percentage of the money you hope to receive. In other words, you should pay for effort in terms of the effort and for the results in terms of the results. Do not pay a percentage of a promise, in advance.*

Stock prices: what do you charge?

You are free to charge as much for your stock as you can get, provided all material facts are disclosed to the purchaser. The directors are entitled to set any price at par or above, and in the absence of fraud this price is conclusive. In establishing a selling price the directors should consider:

- Book value (net worth of the company per share).

- Value based on market rather than book (the replacement cost of the company divided by the number of shares).

- Value based on the investment costs. (What would it cost a new start-up to get to the company's present position?)

- Value based on present earnings, using a reasonable price-earnings ratio.

- Value based on next year's earnings.

- Value based on the sale of similar companies or the price of their stock.

The logic for the chosen selling price should be recorded in the minutes of the directors' meeting.

RECAPPING THE CHAPTER

As a business grows its assets also must grow. The size of the plant, the amount of equipment, and the working capital increase somewhat proportionally to the sales level. This growth must be bootstrapped (be paid for out of earnings) or financed externally. Bootstrapping rarely can accommodate more than 15 percent yearly sales growth. Most companies look to the money market.

Once committed to growth, a company cannot turn back without penalty. More people will have been paid, more purchases made, and more things will have been promised to the customers.

Commitment to growth without assured financing has ruined many *successful companies*. It is the successful companies that need the most financing. Be sure you get enough to do the job.

7

HOW TO GET AND KEEP
GOOD PEOPLE

No one who has ever run a business questions the value of getting and keeping good employees. Much has been written on the subject. Theories abound but conclusive answers are scarce. There are as many examples of companies that are successful with the "theory X" technique (authoritative management) as of those who are successful with "theory Y" (participative management). There are also, in each case, as many failures. I am going to stay out of that controversy. A manager must operate in his own way, using his own style. This chapter is going to stress those things that will work, whether you are a tough boss or a persuasive one.

Take heed: *This is your toughest job. Ninety percent of your mistakes will be people mistakes, not business errors.*

HIRING

Somewhere out there in the world is a man (or woman) who will be the perfect fit for that job opening in your company. Can you flush out that person? Probably not. There are too many obstacles. The number of people, their wide geographic distribution, and the probability that the right person will not be interested all work against you in the search. Moreover, it is unlikely that you would recognize him if you met him. His personality might displease you. His nervousness at the interview might discourage you.

After all, you hire those people with whom you relate. Yet your best choice probably is a person with whom you would clash. What you will do is pick someone who sells himself at the interview, provided his background and references are adequate. As you will pick someone you will like, you will find it more difficult to fire him if he is unsuited. This is a dilemma all managers face.

The best choice

Hire someone you have worked with in the past. He may not be the best man for the job, but he will probably be your best choice. If you do not know such a man, ask a business associate whose judgment you respect. Personal references seem to provide the most suitable candidates. You can see, of course, that this method eliminates from consideration all but a small fraction of the potential candidates.

The search

If you must hire an unknown, do it systematically. Write down the job description, the characteristics you think appropriate for a person holding that job, and the minimum requirements of experience and education. For example:

NATIONAL SALES MANAGER

Job Description

Manage the sales force, including the manufacturers' representatives.

Help prepare the marketing plan.

Set sales quotas by district and product.

Administer the selling-expense budget.

Train and motivate the salesmen.

Contact key accounts and close large sales.

Supervise internal-sales personnel.

Personal Characteristics

"Sales" personality

Honest, straightforward

Ability to communicate clearly

Tough. Able to command respect and obedience of sales force.

Creative. Able to meet goals.

Not given to making excuses

Background

Supervisory sales experience

Formal training in salesmanship

Bachelors degree in marketing or business administration.

Knowledge of product and industry

Successful record in sales

References to Check

Former supervisors

Associates and subordinates

Customer buyers and engineers

Select two or three other people within your company to participate with you in the search. Have them go over the list for omissions or errors. Tell them you want the candidate checked on every point.

Divide the task of checking references among your associates. Use the reference list provided by the candidate but try to come up with at least as many on your own. Particularly try to find people who worked for the candidate. They will have an excellent knowledge of his shortcomings and may be more candid than former supervisors.

Have each one of your associates interview the prospect privately, then record his opinion before he discusses it with anyone else. After each of you has had a turn at an interview, get together for the final evaluation. Listen to whatever is said and then make up your own mind.

Remember: *Each of the interviewers, including you, will have prejudices. Each will view the applicant in the light of his own job. There will be a tendency to downgrade anyone who appears to be a threat.*

No formal personnel department or battery of psychological tests will work any better than this technique. Yet, both what the candidate says and what you heard him to say will differ from the facts. That is why you will make many mistakes.

Finding candidates

There are many adequate ways of turning up applicants with suitable backgrounds. Advertising in the local newspaper, a trade publication, or the *Wall Street Journal* may result in more résumés than you can process.

If the position is for a scarce specialty, an executive search firm may be able to help. It will be able to pluck a man out of a competitor's inner sanctum. However, executive search firms may charge you as much as 20 percent of the man's salary, more than you might be capable of paying. In most cases, particularly when prospects are plentiful, such firms will not be able to do any better than you in finding the right man.

What kind of people should you have?

If you believe in encouraging conflict, mix your people. Do not have any rigid policies like promotion from within or no transfer without the supervisor's approval. Fill key jobs both from inside the company and with new hires. Use young people and mature people. Do not have a mandatory retirement date, but do not let a manager hold the same job for more than five years.

One of the largest independent accounting firms in California uses female accountants exclusively. This firm does not mix its employees, but it does take advantage of a fertile source of talent that has been neglected by other accounting firms.

Set the ground rules when you hire

The best time to tell an employee what he must do and the rules he must follow is before you make him an offer. It should be written down. Even small companies can prepare personnel manuals. If an employee knows what to expect, he will not resent what might otherwise appear to be demeaning.

A large Los Angeles restaurant has a separate locker room with an outside entrance for employees. They must deposit bags and purses in their lockers before entering the restaurant. Nothing can be taken from the restaurant, not even table scraps for dogs. There is no exception to this rule. Employees accept it because it is written in the personnel manual and was made known before they were hired. Had it been imposed after hiring, the employees would have taken it as a slur. Although theft is a major cause for dismissal in the restaurant business, this firm has a low turnover.

If you want to curb personal phone calls, absenteeism, smoking, horseplay, hanky-panky between employees, accepting gratuities, etc., make your rules known in the hiring process.

GETTING THE MOST OUT OF EMPLOYEES

Volumes have been written on motivation. There are many theories on behavior, some very astute and all with some element of truth. This is intended to be a practical book, however, and it is a fact that most small businessmen have neither the time nor the inclination to configure their companies to suit their employees' hierarchy of needs.

So I am going to home in on two simple points. Your employees will work harder and be more satisfied with their jobs if they have *pride* in their accomplishments and *faith* in you.

Pride

You know about pride. It is what coaches strive for. It makes winners out of losers. Your employees must have it if their work is to be good.

Pride takes us back to product, the subject of chapter 5. Your product is the source of your employees' pride. After all, the surroundings are not of their making. Business profits and dividends to stockholders produce little enthusiasm. Only service to the customer produces pride, and there is something of the-chicken-or-the-egg phenomenon here.

Companies that deliver schlock products never have proud employees. If the owner permits poor quality to go out the door, he deprives himself of employee loyalty.

Bringing out the pride

It is not enough to have a good product. Your employees must know it is good and must feel that they have contributed to it. The way to get this across is through praise. Not only your praise for a job well done but the customer's praise for a fine product.

Get the word around. Ask your customer to say something to your employees when he is in your shop. Show people how their work contributes to the whole.

Responsibility contributes to pride. That is just one more reason why delegation of responsibility and authority is important.

Warning: *Peer-group ridicule is the destroyer of pride. Do not tolerate attitudes that detract from worker performance.*

Faith

Your own actions regulate your employees' sense of security. Each employee wants to believe that you will lead the company competently and that you will be wise enough to recognize his worth and fair enough to reward him for his performance. Therefore, you must make decisions objectively and logically and must act with consistency so that your reactions can be predicted. You must encourage those things that help to reach the company's goal and express displeasure at those things that do not.

In 1955, Dr. William Shockley, the inventor of the transistor, started his own company, the Shockley Transistor Corporation. Working for him were most of the people in the country who knew anything about transistors. All of these men stood in awe of Dr. Shockley.

For his own reasons, Shockley decided to concentrate the company's efforts on four-layer diodes rather than transistors. As a result, eight of his key scientists left to form the Fairchild semiconductor division and to produce transistors. Dr. Shockley referred to them as the "traitorous eight." Why did he lose their loyalty? Because they lost their faith in him.

Consistency

Unless you have turned them off, your employees will try to please you. If you are consistent they will know what you want. When you set goals you must measure progress according to those goals. If you set standards you must insist they be met. If you can force yourself to be consistent you will make it easy to work for you, even though your standards are high.

Act consistently

Lip service is not enough. Actions foster belief.

The president of a large company was consistently stressing in his talks and intracompany memos the need for economy. Yet he based the company's salary structure on the number of people the managers had working for them. Result? He created a company of empire builders.

Another chief executive, while giving lip service to product quality, spent most of his time reviewing shipping status and never looked at the condition of the equipment as it left the plant. As a result, his employees pushed defective items out the door to meet production schedules.

Still another president, of a delivery-plagued electronics manufacturing firm, made a practice of filling key managerial openings out of the ranks of the project engineers, whether or not they had a good record for completing their assignments on time. The company is plagued by late shipments because nobody takes the schedules seriously.

Actions are more important than what you say. If you promote people who agree with you, you will have a company full of yes-men. If you treat poor workmanship as natural and unavoidable, you will have a poor quality product. If you accept excuses, you will get them. Your employees will give you what your actions say you want.

People play the game to get high scores

The Vietnam War was an excellent illustration of the scoring syndrome. When the president put pressure on the military to win the war, the army came up with the body-count. Every week they listed the number of Vietcong bodies they buried. After a while they added innocent bystanders, dead cats and dogs, and perhaps some vivid tales. The air force, not to be outdone, invented the sortie an airplane flight with a bomb drop. A bomb dropped on a tree was just as much a sortie as a bomb dropped on a bridge or an enemy column.

Of course, neither body-counts nor sorties had anything to do with winning the war. The determination of the North Vietnamese to fight on, the crucial element, was immeasurable.

As president of the company you want profit and perhaps growth. That is all. Do not get caught in the trap of counting secondary objectives. If you count shipments only, quality will suffer. if you call for cost reductions, shipments can suffer. Your people will score according to your rules.

Bill Russell probably was the most effective basketball player of all time, yet he was not a high scorer. He just won games. When Wilt Chamberlain started playing like Russell, his scores went down but his teams won more games. Your people must know that profits are what you want, not efficient departments. They must cooperate to meet the team goal and some departments must spend effort bolstering others.

Communications

Communication is a two-way transaction. Whether you are a manager who hands down decisions from the top or are one who builds from the roots, what matters most is whether your people listen to one another. You must build an atmosphere where people feel free to talk up and know they will be heard. If you do this, the company will have communications.

Every question deserves an answer, and every suggestion should be received with gratitude. People who ask questions and make suggestions are trying to help, even if their motives are self-serving. If allowed to develop, this becomes a source of added power. As the sports writers like to say, it gives you an added dimension.

Fairness

It should be obvious that you should treat every employee with fairness, even if it is not possible to treat them all alike.

Compensation

Relative compensation is more important than actual. Your chief engineer may be making 50 percent less than the national average and be perfectly happy, but let him discover that the controller makes $2,000 a year more and all hell breaks lose.

Good young executives are never satisfied with their rate of pay for very long, regardless of the circumstances. So you have to keep things in balance and you have to give periodic increases. Still, everyone will not be happy. It is a juggling act without a handy set of instructions. Sorry 'bout that.

Profit participation

Some companies have had remarkable success with profit-sharing plans. Lincoln Electric is a prime example. The companies that are successful are the ones that have profits to share.

The marginal companies that install profit-sharing plans as a cure for their managerial shortcomings are always disappointed. I have never seen a company go from loss to profit position as a result of a profit-sharing plan.

Profit sharing has to be companywide if it is to qualify for tax advantages. Bonuses that amount to the same thing, but have no tax advantages, may be passed out according to whim. Executive bonuses are commonplace and probably do contribute to company earnings, but IBM, which has never been lacking for profits, passes out few, if any bonuses.

Stock options

In the 1950s, stock options were eagerly sought. Since then they have lost much of their glamor. In small publicly held companies there are still large gains to be made on stock options, so some plan should be instituted. Before the company goes public, they make little sense.

Consider compensation a secondary factor

Although the form and amount of compensation that is best for your company is a very nebulous thing, it is a secondary morale factor, provided the wages you pay are adequate and reasonably competitive. Don't lose too much sleep over it and do not be talked into any far-out scheme. As the company grows in size and in earnings, pay higher salaries. Your employees will get the message.

How about the guy who does not fit?

The most common managerial error is retaining people who cannot do their jobs. Large companies go to the extreme of institutionalizing this mistake, by moving the square pegs around to see whether there are holes they will fit.

A small business absolutely cannot afford this luxury. If you have such a man, take a deep breath and tell him goodbye. The sooner the better, for both of you.

One final word on this. Never hang on to a man because he appears to be essential. You cannot afford to have such an employee or such a business. If you do, sell it to him and start something else.

HANDLING CREATIVE PEOPLE

Employee relations is your toughest job, and handling creative people the toughest part of it. If you are concerned that you have not been able to solve this problem, concern yourself no more. You will always have it and there is no permanent solution, only a series of day-to-day temporizing measures. A large majority of the highly creative individuals who make up fields of fashion, entertainment, and advertising, and even a large portion of research scientists have personalities that cannot be placated for very long.

What creative employees mean to you

You put up with creative people for one reason: they make your product superior. If you are in such a situation you probably recognize this fact and are willing to go out of your way to satisfy these people. Unfortunately, they have a way of destroying the morale of your sane employees. There are times when you must choose between keeping a valuable and talented individual and keeping the rest of your organization. Try to avoid this kind of showdown at all costs.

Treat them with good humor

Some broad humor with a touch of deference is a device that has worked well for several managers I have observed.

"Hey, do you think our mathematical genius can fill out a time card?" is a better approach than a straight request. If the rest of the company goes along with the gag, there is an all-around slacking off of tension. Unfortunately, some talented people are too sensitive to be joshed. This technique has its limitations.

Always remember this: it's not a question of whether she is a prima donna. It's a question of how well she sings.

Finally: if you control them, you destroy them.

UNIONS AND HOW TO DO WITHOUT THEM

Whether you think unions are a necessary ingredient in a democratic, capitalistic society or become paranoid at the very mention of them, you must agree that a small company is better off without one. It is quite possible to keep them out or, if you already have a union, to get them out.

Why employees sign up with unions

In some towns, unions are traditional with laborers. The worker signs the card because his father is a union man and his brother is a union man and he would not think of voting against the union. If you are in such a town, make peace with the union officials and learn to live with them. Fighting will drain too much of your energy.

If you are in an area where the unions are not taken for granted, whether your employees sign up with one depends on what they think of you and how they think you feel about a union.

If your company is a good place to work, there is little a union can offer except increased wages. If your company has many senseless rules, it is ripe for union infiltration.

The worst kinds of rules are those that have little or nothing to do with the job or the welfare of the employees as a whole. Dress restrictions or hair style rules might fit in this category. Such rules are made to satisfy your prejudices and therefore are apt to be resented.

The best thing to do is to provide for employees little extras that could not be enforced by a union contract. One company that has been successful in countless union elections helps employees in their personal battles with the merchants in town, getting bad merchandise replaced and stalled service under way—little things that indicate management *cares*.

Some rules for keeping the union out

Do not have merit increases at the factory level. Treat everyone exactly the same. The pay scale should be a function of seniority.

Do not take away privileges without explaining why it is necessary to do so.

Do not make any caste system too obvious. Of course, higher-level people may have extra privileges, but do not have empty slots in the executive parking lot if many workers have to pay for their own parking at commercial lots.

Let your people know how you feel about unions. Not on a personal level, but how unions will affect your business. Believe it or not, a lot of people think the boss does not care one way or the other.

The final rule is the most important. Get rid of marginal producers quickly. Marginal people are the biggest instigators and also cause the most discontent among the conscientious workers. Nothing is more discouraging than to see a goof-off making as much as they are.

What to do when the union shows up at your door

At the first sign of union activity, get yourself a lawyer who specializes in antiunion activities. Go out of town to get one, if necessary. A general practitioner will not suffice. When you have located such a specialist, follow his advice.

First aid until you get an attorney

- Don't accept any sign-up cards from union representatives.
- Do not talk to any union representative.
- Do not allow any union representative in your plant.
- Make no promises or threats to any employee, and make no statement that could be interpreted later as a promise or threat.
- Put a gag on your supervisors. Tell them, most emphatically, not to discuss the organizing attempt.
- Put a hold on all disciplinary actions.

Isn't there anything you can do?

There are lots of things you can do to combat unionism, but one improper statement can result in a victory by default. That is why you must be guided by an attorney who knows the rules and all of the tricks.

What is the National Labor Relations Board?

The NLRB is an independent federal agency established by the National Labor Relations Act of 1935 amended by the

Taft-Hartley Act of 1947 and the Landrum-Griffin Act of 1959. Its charter is to conduct elections related to representation and to make determinations on unfair labor practices. It is empowered to remedy unfair acts but not to punish or force admissions of guilt.

Steps leading to organization

For the union to become the bargaining agent for your employees, it must establish itself by agreement of the employer or by winning a majority vote in an election or by NLRB edict when the employer is guilty of serious unfair acts.

The first step in organization is getting the workers to sign authorization cards.

It is improper for the union to solicit card signatures on company property during working hours. However, signatures can be sought during coffee breaks and lunch periods. If the company has a rule banning all solicitations on company property, including charitable collections, it can bar a union campaigning for card signatures on any company property.

A petition signed by workers also is a satisfactory form of establishing union recognition.

NLRB elections

If 30 percent or more of the employees sign a petition or authorization cards, the union can submit a "petition" for election" form to the regional office of the NLRB.

The NLRB will send a copy of the petition to the employer, who can challenge votes.

The NLRB will not conduct an election unless it covers all employees in an appropriate bargaining unit. This can be all members of a particular trade or all employees at a discrete location.

The employer must also meet certain requirements. If the business is a retail store, annual sales must be $500,000 or more. Other types of businesses must have annual purchases of $50,000 or more from out-of-state suppliers.

If everything is in order, the NLRB will docket the election and assign a field examiner. It will send a notice to employees telling them of their rights.

No election will be held if there is a contract in effect. This is called the *contract bar rule*. It applies to companies that already have an established union.

The NLRB will ask union and employer to sign an election "consent" form. This gives the regional director broad powers to determine whether there has been any improper conduct and to establish voting eligibility.

Another form stipulates that the regional director has investigative powers but that the board makes the final decision.

If both sides do not consent to the election, the regional director will hold a hearing and within a month thereafter will make a decision in writing.

After an election has been ordered

Seven days after an election has been directed or consented to, the employer must supply the NLRB with a list of all eligible employees' names and addresses. This is called the *Excelsior List*. This list is distributed to all parties for use in campaigning.

Supervisors cannot contact employees at their homes, but union organizers may. If the company holds meetings for a captive audience the union may request equal time.

Prior to the election, the company and the union can select observers to monitor the election.

Following the election

Within five days after the election, either side may file objections regarding eligibility of voters or unfair labor practices. If the union is found guilty of unfair practices, the election may be ordered reheld. If the employer is guilty, there may be another election or the employer may be ordered to recognize the union as the bargaining agent for the employees.

Recognition by agreement

A union with authorization cards for more than half of the employees may request that the employer recognize it as the bargaining agent. If the union makes such a claim or demand, the employer can insist on an election unless he commits a serious unfair labor practice or unless he has by some act acquiesced to the union demand.

Employer petition

The employer, on demand of the union, may petition the NLRB for an election. This can be done in writing or by telephone. It is necessary to execute the "petition for election" form, however, before the NLRB will docket the election.

Decertification

Employees can rid themselves of a union by getting 30 percent to sign a petition for an election to decertify. The petition must say:

"We, the employees of the _____ company, desire that the NLRB conduct an election to determine whether the _____ union continue to represent employees."

It should be signed and dated by 30 percent of the employees.

It is illegal for the management of any corporation to assist the employees in any such decertification attempt. However, when the management believes the union no longer represents the employees, and has facts to back up this belief, it may submit a petition for decertification election. A statement of the facts must accompany the petition.

Employer unfair practices

The following is a sample of unfair labor practices that may be charged against the employer:

- Interference, restraint, and coercion.
- Discrimination.
- Unlawful assistance to the union.
- Refusal to bargain (with an authorized representative).
- Promises.

Union unfair practices

The unions also can be guilty of unfair practices, although the NLRB has often been accused of lacking enthusiasm in the policing of union activities. Here are some illegal union actions:

- Restraint and coercion.
- Violence, threats, and mass picketing.
- Discrimination.
- Secondary boycotts and jurisdictional disputes.
- Excessive dues.
- Featherbedding.
- Refusal to bargain.

Fight strikes

Do not cave in if your employees go out on strike. It is possible to break a strike, and in some cases it is necessary. The tactics will depend on your circumstances. Your attorney should show you the way.

RECAPPING THE CHAPTER

People retain in their minds few things at any one time. This chapter is not a reference for use when you need it. You have to live it. So, what should you remember?

- Build pride.
- Be consistent.
- Listen.
- Cull marginal performers.

8

HOW TO SELL

This book is not going to tell you anything about salesmanship. There are many excellent books on that subject at your local bookstore or library. Instead, this chapter will show you how to marshall your forces to maximize your salesman's effectiveness.

Marketing

Some people refer to the total selling effort as *marketing,* to distinguish it from those things done by salesmen alone. Thus we have marketing managers and marketing plans. The dictionary does not make any distinction. I use *marketing* and *selling* interchangeably, because selling is always more than confronting the customer and asking for his order.

Nothing happens till you make a sale.

As was previously explained, the two tasks of a company are making and selling. Of the two, selling is the more difficult because the customer is outside the company's span of control. You cannot order a prospect to buy something, yet without that sale the company cannot exist. The salesman is the agent that activates the customer. He works for you, theoretically, but he, too, is outside your absolute control. You

can order him to produce. You can send him out on the road.
You can teach him good selling techniques. But you cannot
make him sell.

What a salesman sells

When he is face to face with a prospect, a salesman can sell
the product, the company, or himself. Any one of those may
make the sale. All three improve the odds.

He will sell what he believes in. No more than that. His
belief will not come from within, except perhaps his self-
belief. You and the rest of your employees must provide
that belief.

Roles

We think of a salesman as selling the customer and working
for his company or his principal. We think of the customer as
a buyer, not a seller. The relationships are more complex,
however. Roles can be multiple. The company must sell its
salesman. The customer may sell the company's salesman.
The salesman may really work for the customer. The salesman
may own the customer.

Selling the salesman

The company whose products are handled by manufacturers'
representatives must convince each rep salesman to spend as
much time as possible selling its products, regardless of the
commissions he earns from his other lines. In that respect the
other lines carried by the reps are the company's primary
competition.

The company must also sell its own salesman on working
harder and selling with more confidence. It must sell him on
the company, on the product, and on himself.

Selling the product to the salesman

If your product is good, you must make certain your salesman
knows why. Behind every product is a body of knowledge.
Top-notch salesmen will find this out for themselves, buy why
make them work for it? Make it easy for them to understand

what they are selling by giving them some of your expertise. Hold classes. Write sales manuals. Have group discussions.

In a retail store there are often more products than can be studied comprehensively, but certainly some can. Besides, the true product may be trust or convenience. The salesman can be taught how to project trust and what convenience means in terms of customer shopping habits.

Do not assume that the salesman knows your products. Many salesmen fake it. Take the time to teach him.

Selling the salesman on the company

A salesman will believe in his company if it does what it says it will do. That is really all it takes. When a salesman is on the road he cannot worry about what the company is doing. He must know that if you promised delivery for Wednesday you will deliver on Wednesday or clear it with the customer without being asked. He must know that if you promised a serviceman, he will show up, and that if you promised information, it will be in the mail.

To sell a salesman on the company you must convince your employees that his needs are important. If your in-plant people support him, his trust in the company increases. Only actions count. Unfilled promises cannot be explained away.

Things to do

Log in every call and every memo from field salesmen. See that they are answered within a prescribed time, like twenty-four hours, *without fail*. If the exact information is not available, a promise date is given but the communication is *answered*. Take a personal interest in this. Accept no excuses.

Do not allow anyone to assume that the salesman does not know what he is talking about and therefore has no problem. The salesman may not know what he is talking about and he may have incorrectly identified the problem, but he would not have called if everything was all right.

Give customer business top priority. Do not get upset when a customer walks in and makes you lose your inventory count. Within reason, put other things aside to help your salesman land an order or a new customer.

Selling the salesman on himself

A salesman's self-image determines his performance. Some salesmen are naturally high on themselves, but most have a need for outside reassurance. The best way for you to make them believe they are important is to think and act that way. When your overprotective secretary blocks a salesman's incoming phone call, he knows how he stacks up. If the switchboard operator does not even know who he is but asks his company affiliation, he knows what his fellow employees think of his job.

The president of a small household appliance company frequently toured the country calling on key accounts. He usually ignored the individual salesman but was accompanied by the owner of the rep organization in that territory. He used to brag that it took his personal appearance to get things going. Rep salesmen were unproductive, he complained. He never bothered to explain how some of them made large commissions selling their other lines.

Things to do

Make sure key employees in all departments know the names of the salesmen. Have them call the salesmen with important information. The more employees who have personal contact with outside sales personnel, the better the internal support will be.

Set up pigeonholes at some convenient location with the salesmen's names on them. Encourage people to drop handwritten notes in these pigeonholes. Scoop up the contents at the end of each day and put them in the mail.

Instruct all secretaries to pass on sales calls without interrogation.

Keep a list of a sales personnel at the switchboard. Make sure the operator knows where to refer calls.

If you have good news, give it to the salesman to pass on to the customer.

If the news is bad, have someone in authority let the customer know. A call from the manufacturing manager reporting on a late delivery and promising a new date is much more reassuring than one from the sales clerk.

The salesman works for the customer

If a salesman's loyalty sometimes seems divided, that is because it is. A salesman's major asset is the customers he "owns." When a salesman owns a customer it means the customer believes in him and will buy from him. He can sell this asset to others besides yourself. He will not give this up easily. He will work for the customer, to keep him as an asset, as hard as he works for the person who pays his wages.

The salesman sells the company

Just as the company sells the salesman on working harder for the company, the salesman sells the company on working harder for his customer. His competition is your other customers.

The customer will also sell him in order to get more out of you, like lower prices or faster delivery.

Know who your salesmen really are

Some retail stores require people skilled in salesmanship. Stores selling clothing, furniture, appliances, and automobiles are examples.

Some require people who know the product but do not have to convince people to buy. Record shops, bookstores, and sporting goods stores are examples. The sales personnel are there to inform and to serve but not to pressure.

Some are self-service stores. People come in to buy the things they select for themselves.

Each one of these types of stores is selling something, however. A sales job is being done on the customer.

People buy from supermarkets that are clean and well laid out, appealing to the appetite. The salespeople are those who arrange the store, keep the aisles clean, and train the other personnel.

Elsewhere it may be the window-display man or the advertising copywriter or the costume designer.

Do the stewardesses sell airplane tickets? Ask Singapore Airlines.

The person who cleans your restrooms could be one of your most important salesmen.

Everybody sells

When an employee talks to a friend about his job he could be making a sale. Make sure your employees know all about your company and its products.

People who buy for your firm contact other companies every day. They transmit a picture of your company every time they make a phone call. Do not let them treat vendors with arrogance.

Engineers and quality control personnel can be excellent salesmen in their normal business relationships with other companies.

Selling a service

If there is no tangible product associated with your service or if the product is customized for the individual customer, you must sell the customer on the company and its capability.

Credibility is achieved slowly and lost in a flash. People who buy customized services ask around. Your previous customers are your salesmen, for better or worse. A bad reputation may be impossible to overcome, so do a good job on every order.

Sometimes products sell themselves

If you place your product on the desk of a buyer, he may buy it regardless of your financial condition and the way your factory looks. There ought to be a Latin phrase for it. Like *la productium omnia est.*

Before a customer stakes *his* product on *your* product, he will want to know all about your business. For large-quantity future deliveries, credibility must be provided. Then it is your reputation that sells.

Tools of marketing

If you think you are doing most of the little things that can be done to help sales, refer to the appendix and see how many are not being done. The marketing chores, like a housewife's, are never done.

Advertising

Almost every business can use some form of advertising. Small businesses should stick to advertising the *product,* not the company image (unless that is the product). To learn all you need to know about advertising, try to get a copy of David Ogilvy's *Confessions of an Adman.* This is the best book I have ever read on advertising, and it is a pretty good marketing primer, too.

Selling expenses

It costs money to sell your product. Accounting people classify this money as selling *expense.* This causes no end of confusion.

An expense is a cost of doing business. Accountants like to keep selling expenses bound as a percentage of sales. This may be a valid condition if the selling expenses are related to the actual sales. Quite often this is not the case. The selling expenses generate future sales and therefore are more in the nature of an *investment* than an expense.

An accountant's legitimate interest is in how you pay your bills. Bills get paid not out of future sales but out of past and present sales. So he worries when you exceed the percentage he establishes.

There is nothing wrong, however, with making investments out of today's profits to pay for tomorrow's increased business if that is what you consider to be to your best interest. It is still an investment, whether your accountant calls it an expense or not. Of course you should not carry such an investment on the books as an asset, so it is an expense. But it does build for the future, so it is an investment. You and your accountant are both right, but you do what you want.

9

WHAT YOU MUST KNOW ABOUT BEAN COUNTING

No matter how complicated your business or what kind of mathematics you use in providing your service, its success or failure usually boils down to fourth-grade arithmetic. Do you take in more than you spend? Is your selling price higher than your costs? Do you have enough money to see you through? You must know enough about accounting to get those answers.

What is accounting, anyway?

Accounting is a systematized method of keeping score. It is meant to reveal but it has been used to deceive.

Accounting can help you manage your resources. It can warn you of cash shortages and help you find financing. It measures your success and gives your business status and respectability.

Accounting is far from an exact science, but it is a precise manipulator. It will take any amount of numbers and put them into prearranged categories, modify them as programmed, and hand them back to you. Because certain numbers such as cash in the bank and debts owed are verifiable and indisputable, it is possible to make the accounting system self-correcting over long periods of time. If the categories and the modifiers are consistent, the numbers you get will begin to make sense and will become useful tools.

Limitations of accounting

Accounting is taught in business schools, but that does not mean that accountants are businessmen.

Accounting may tell you whether you have made a profit, but accounting does not make profits. Profits are made by selling a service at the right price.

Your accountant may tell you (correctly) that your price is too low, but he cannot make people buy it at a higher price.

Over a long period of time, accounting can tell you reliably whether your company has made money and how much. It can tell you which parts of your business contributed most to your profits, but the validity of this information depends upon the method for allocating costs, and accounting systems have severe limitations in this regard. Many apparently cost-accounting systems give deceptive results because the expenses are attributed to the wrong causes.

General accounting

General accounting is the term applied to the accumulation of records, their sifting and collating, and their translation into the financial statements of the business. The collection and sorting of these records is referred to as bookkeeping. Every company must keep books that record the transactions in that company and with the outside world. This includes monies received and paid out, invoices received and sent out, goods and services received and performed.

Cash and accrual methods

Cash accounting is the most basic system. Revenues are not recognized until the money is received. Expenses are recorded as paid, rather than as incurred.

Uneducated immigrants with little knowledge of accounting have had astounding success in running profitable businesses. They used a special version of cash accounting sometimes called *mom and pop* accounting. Once their meager savings are put into the store fixtures and initial inventory, nothing new is ordered until the money is in the cash register. Money left at the end of the month goes to pay for living expenses. If the monthly residual is too low, prices are raised. If sales drop, prices are lowered. The willingness of the proprietor to adjust his standard of living gives the business the cushion it needs to weather hard times. It is a simple system and it works. The more your accounting system differs from mom and pop accounting, the less you will know about the reality of your profits.

The *accrual* method of accounting is used by most companies because it has look-ahead features. Sales are recorded when invoiced, even though no payment has been received. Liabilities are recorded when bills or invoices are received.

Financial statements

The purpose of all the record keeping is the company's financial statements. These show the financial strength of the company and its earnings over the most recent period. They are required for income tax purposes and for obtaining loans and investments. A financial statement is made up of the balance sheet and the operating (or profit and loss) statement.

THE BALANCE SHEET

A balance sheet is a statement of financial condition at a particular time. It is called a "balance" sheet because the number at the bottom of the left-hand side must equal the number at the bottom of the right-hand side. This is a result of the *accounting equation*: assets equal liabilities plus equity. Many people have a hard time comprehending the accounting equation because it is constructed as an identity. All it says is that a business's worth is equal to what it owns less what it owes. Figure 9-1 is an example of a balance sheet.

Assets

The assets of a company are the things it owns or has a right to. Assets are evaluated according to accounting rules. These rules tend to minimize the value of the assets because accounting principles were established primarily to protect creditors and investors from deception.

Assets are also categorized or grouped under various headings.

Current assets

Current assets are those that are liquid or nearly liquid. Cash, accounts receivable, negotiable securities, debts collectible in the current year, and prepaid bills and inventories comprise current assets. Current assets are adjusted downward for contingencies like doubtful accounts.

Fixed assets

Fixed assets are land, building, and equipment, including leasehold improvements and office furnishings.

Other assets

Other assets are those that do not fit into either of the other two categories, like design rights, patent costs, organization costs, deferred expenses, and good will.

Tangible and intangible assets

Tangible assets are those with a definite value, like the land and building. Intangible assets are those that are nebulous because of unpredictability. For example, patent costs are intangible because the patent may turn out to be of little or no value. Leasehold improvements are intangible because their value reverts to the landlord at the expiration of the lease. You do not have to decide for yourself what is tangible and what is not. Any CPA can tell you. The American Institute of Certified Public Accountants defines what is intangible.

Inventory

Inventory is items held for future sale. Stationery, ledgers, toilet paper, and towels are not inventory. They are *supplies*.

Figure 9-1/Hardgoods Manufacturing Company/Balance Sheet as of July 1, 197-

ASSETS

CURRENT ASSETS:

Cash	$ 25,000	
Securities	5,000	
Accounts receivable (trade)	208,000	
Other receivables and notes due	20,000	
Inventories:		
Finished goods	65,000	
Work in process	110,000	
Raw materials and purchased parts	45,000	
Prepaid expenses	11,000	
Total current assets	$489,000	

PROPERTY, PLANT, AND EQUIPMENT:

(Cost, $425,000, less accumulated depreciation of $250,000)	$175,000

OTHER ASSETS:

Patent costs	$ 20,000	
Deferred debt expense	45,000	
Deferred development costs	12,000	
Total other assets	$ 77,000	

TOTAL ASSETS	$741,000

LIABILITIES

CURRENT LIABILITIES:

Notes payable	$ 29,000	
Accounts payable (trade)	117,000	
Accrued expenses	14,000	
Deferred taxes	18,000	
Total current liabilities	$178,000	

LONG-TERM DEBT:

8% ten-year note	$ 63,000	
Subordinated convertible debentures	100,000	
Mortgage	140,000	
Total liabilities	$481,000	

EQUITY

100 shares common stock @ $100 par	$ 10,000	
Additional paid-in capital	90,000	
Retained earnings	160,000	
Total stockholder equity	$260,000	

TOTAL LIABILITIES AND EQUITY	$741,000

Supplies are not valued on the balance sheet. They are expensed as though they are consumed upon receipt.

Inventory is valued at the lower of cost or market. This is an accounting rule.

If the inventory is goods held for resale, as it is in most retail establishments, the cost is the purchase price.

If the inventory was manufactured, its cost is the labor, material, and other manufacturing expenses required to produce it. These other expenses are called *manufacturing overhead* and require a system of prorating such things as supervision, factory supplies, rent, depreciation, and utilities against the production output.

Work in a semicompleted state also is inventory. It is called *work in process*.

Whenever the cost of the inventory exceeds the reasonably anticipated sales price (called market value), the value of the inventory is reduced to the market value. This results in a reduction of profits for the period in which the adjustment was made.

Any inventory that has been kept in the stockroom for over a year may be devalued or entirely written off. This is an accounting rule to prevent obsolete or slow-moving inventory from inflating the value of the company.

Can a company that is in a service business with no tangible product have any inventory? The answer is yes. Labor and associated expenses for jobs in progress is recorded as work in process inventory. Of course there is no finished goods inventory or raw material inventory.

FIFO

Inventory costs can be determined by FIFO or LIFO methods. FIFO means first in, first out. Because the purchase price of goods is constantly changing, there must be a system of evaluation that can be maintained from year to year. The FIFO system establishes that the item sold is the earliest one purchased. The inventory remaining in stock is therefore valued at the latest purchase prices. If prices are rising, this means that the inventory value is based on the recent high prices and the goods sold at the earlier, lower prices.

LIFO

The last in, first out method uses the earliest prices for inventory evaluation and the latest prices for the cost of goods sold. This is a more conservative method of accounting.

Figure 9-2 shows the way FIFO and LIFO affect the company's financial statements

Inventory count

Although there are many methods for keeping track of inventory through record keeping, it is an accounting practice (and an audit requirement) that a physical count be made for the year-end closing of the books. The inventory should be stocked in a way to make counting easy, and the purchase price of all inventory must be readily available for the accountant's review. In many retail stores the item's cost is coded on the item ticket. There are many commonly used codes for such information. See figure 9-3.

Fixed assets

Fixed assets are valued at *book*. Book is the cost less the accumulated depreciation. The capital equipment you own may be worth more than what you paid for it, but you cannot show that value on the books. On the other hand, if the reasonable market value is lower than your book value, you may make a downward adjustment.

Depreciation

Every fixed asset except land is depreciated according to some schedule. Its value is reduced as a function of time until it reaches zero or some low salvage price. Buildings are usually depreciated over twenty years, heavy equipment over five to ten years, and light equipment and furnishings over three to five.

Intangibles are depreciated according to their expected useful life. For example, product development costs may be depreciated over the anticipated sales period of the product, and leasehold improvements depreciated over the life of the lease.

Purchase record for Stock #53—Man's suit, style wr:

1 March purchased 20 @ $ 70.00 ea. = $1,400 total
1 May   purchased 20 @   90.00 ea. = 1,800 total
1 July   purchased 20 @   100.00 ea. = 2,000 total

On 1 July, Fitrite had sold a total of 30 suits, 20 @ $120 each and 10 @ 140 each.

Using the FIFO method

The 30 suits remaining in inventory are worth 10 × $90 + 20 × $100 = $2,900.

The cost of sales for the suits sold = 20 × $70 + 10 × $90 = $2,300.

Sales were 20 × $120 + 10 × $140 = $3,800.

Gross profit is $3,800 − $2,300 = $1,500.

Using the LIFO method

The 30 suits remaining in inventory are worth 10 × $90 + 20 × $70 = $2,300.

Cost of sales for the suits sold = 10 × $90 + 20 × $100 = $2,900.

Gross profit is $3,800 − $2,900 = $900.

The operating statement shows $600 less profit and the balance sheet shows $600 lower inventory value when LIFO is used.

Figure 9-2/Fitrite Clothing Store/FIFO vs LIFO

```
1 2 3 4 5 6 7 8 9 0
M A K E P R O F I T
```

Examples: **KIIP** = $ 39.95
ATT = 2.00
MEPTT = 145.00

Item: Lamp
Stock #7328
Price $79.00

KITT

Figure 9-3/Sample Code for Noting Item Cost on Floor Ticket

If the depreciation is the same every year, it is referred to as *straight line* depreciation. If the depreciation is greater in the early years, it is called accelerated depreciation. Because depreciation reduces profits without reducing cash flow, the IRS looks carefully at accelerated depreciation and requires that it be justified by the facts.

The theory behind depreciation is that the business must put aside funds to replace worn equipment. In practice, many companies use equipment that has had zero book value for many years.

Liabilities

Liabilities are obligations to pay money or provide services. These include all borrowings, invoices for goods received for which payment has not been made (accounts payable), salaries and wages due, taxes incurred, and reserves for possible losses or claims. A liability must be shown as soon as it is recognized, even though the liability has not yet become a fact. Reserves for losses in litigation must be set up unless, in the opinion of the company's counsel, the suit against the company is entirely without merit.

Obligations due within the year are called *current liabilities*. All others are long-term liabilities. The difference between current assets and current liabilities is *working capital*.

Equity

The equity section of the balance sheet shows the net worth of the business. It is composed of the money that has been invested in the company and the money that has been earned by the company from its inception. This latter figure, called *retained earnings*, can be negative, which would show that the company has had accumulative losses. It is also possible for the net worth to be negative, although only a very sick company would be in such a condition.

Accountants have rules about the treatment of capital on the balance sheet and about separating investments into capital and surplus. These rules are not germaine to the running of your business.

THE OPERATING STATEMENT

Whereas the balance sheet is a statement of condition at a particular time, the operating statement is a report of results over a specified period, like a month, quarter, or year. The most basic of operating statements is depicted in figure 9-4. This statement applies to any type of business, but it shows very little detail. To provide enough information to allow for some analysis, an expanded statement is required. Operating statements will vary, depending on the type of business.

Operating statement for a merchandising business

Figure 9-5 shows a statement for a typical clothing store. From it you can see how much was spent on new purchases, how the inventory changed, and what the major expenses were. By itself it provides little information, but when compared with prior statements it reveals trends that could be important.

Operating statement for a restaurant

Figure 9-6 shows how a restaurant statement could look. The important feature of this statement is the separation of the

Net sales	$644,350
Cost of goods sold	510,785
Gross profit	133,565
Other expenses	64,200
Profit before provision for taxes	69,365
Provision for taxes	35,000
Net profit	$ 34,365

Figure 9-4 Zen Company/Operating Statement/
For the Year Ended December 31, 197-

Net sales	$720,000
Cost of goods sold:	
Beginning inventory	100,000
Items purchased	520,000
Less ending inventory	(130,000)
Total	490,000
Gross profit	230,000
Expenses:	
Salaries and commissions	108,000
Costs of occupancy	12,000
Selling and advertising	10,000
Other expenses	15,000
Total	145,000
Profit before provision for taxes	85,000
Provision for taxes	40,000
Net profit	$45,000

Figure 9-5 Excel Clothiers/Operating Statement/
For the Year Ended September 30, 197-

cost of sales for the food and the bar portions of the business. This separation allows the owner to watch for waste or theft and to take corrective action quickly.

Manufacturers

Manufacturers perform more functions than do other types of businesses and their operating statements are therefore more complicated. Those expenses that are normally associated with the manufacturing of the product are included in the cost of sales. Such expenses include the cost of the materials and purchased parts that go into the delivered item, the cost of the labor to make it (called *direct labor*), and the associated costs like rent for the factory area, supervision, and factory supplies. These latter costs are the manufacturing overhead. Figure 9–7 shows an operating statement for a manufacturing company.

Overhead rate

You have undoubtedly heard the term used. It is the ratio of the overhead expenses to the direct labor costs. Overhead rate is used in pricing, as a means of allocating these overhead expenses to the various products or contracts. The rate is used also in the evaluation of inventory. Because overhead is allocated against direct labor, many people, including accountants, think that overhead is caused by direct labor. This is not the case.

General, administrative, and selling costs

To complete the operating statement of a manufacturing company, a category for expenses unrelated to manufacturing is required. Sometimes two are used, if selling costs are important enough to be broken out separately. General and administrative expenses is a mouthful, so it is usually shortened to G&A.

The G&A rate

The G&A rate is the ratio of the G&A expenses to the manufacturing costs. It is used in bidding and pricing. G&A

	Food	Bar	Total
Net sales	$550,000	$180,000	$730,000
Cost of food and beverages	175,000	40,000	215,000
Labor	190,000	70,000	260,000
Gross profit	185,000	70,000	255,000

General expenses:

Management salaries	66,000
Occupancy costs	40,000
Licenses, insurance, etc.	20,000
Promotion and advertising	10,000
Other	15,000
Total	151,000
Pretax income	104,000
Provisions for taxes	52,000
Net income	$52,000

Figure 9-6 Gourmet Restaurant Company
Operating Statement For the Year Ended March 31, 197-

Sales	$120,000
Less returns	(1,500)
Net sales	118,500
Beginning inventory	220,000
Direct labor	31,000
Materials and purchased parts	38,000
Manufacturing overhead expenses	35,000
Less ending inventory	(226,000)
Cost of goods sold	98,000
General and administrative expenses	14,000
Total costs	112,000
Pretax operating profit for June	$6,500

Figure 9-7 Hardgoods Manufacturing Company
Operating Statement For the Month of June 197-

expenses are not caused by manufacturing costs, however. Like the overhead rate, the G&A rate is used to pass such costs on to the customer, not to identify the source.

Gross profit

The term gross profit refers to the difference between sales and the cost of sales. It is also called gross margin. Whatever it is, it is not profit. Profit is what is left after all expenses and costs have been deducted from sales.

The bottom line

The last number on an operating statement is the profit. It should be shown after all taxes and after all extraordinary income or losses. There are other kinds of profits: operating profits, pretax profits, and extraordinary income.

Summary

The balance sheet and the operating statement are the primary financial reports of any business. In themselves they supply information of considerable value, as the next chapter will show. However, there are two other numbers that do not show up on any financial statement but should be reported.

Backlog

Backlog is what remains after sales (or shipments) are subtracted from new orders (bookings). It tells you how much work must be done to fill outstanding orders. If you are a wholesaler it tells you how much goods must be shipped. A retailer's backlog is orders he was unable to fill out of stock. It is not an important factor in most retail businesses.

Purchase commitments

This is the inverse of backlog. It is how much you have ordered but not received. It is an important factor in cash management.

Recapping the chapter

You have now learned enough about accounting to use financial reports in the management of your business. Remember, your accountant is not the financial manager, because he only counts the costs. You control them.

10
BY THE NUMBERS

It is better to know a little bit about accounting and use what you know than to know much but not put your knowledge into use. Being able to understand financial statements does not make you an astute financial man, but it does give you a surprising number of tools. Just as physical diseases make themselves known through strange feelings, business diseases may show up as anomalies in the financial statement before they work their way down to the bottom line.

BREAK-EVEN ANALYSIS

The first exercise in number management is determining your company's break-even point: the minimum monthly sales volume required to cover expenses.

Start with a piece of graph paper with the x-axis graduated in dollars of monthly sales. The y-axis should be on the same scale and labeled monthly costs. Plot the best curve you can to match your monthly costs as a function of the monthly sales volume. See figure 10-1. Draw a line from the origin at 45 degrees. This is a line that represents $X = Y$. Where that line crosses the cost-sales curve is the company's break-even

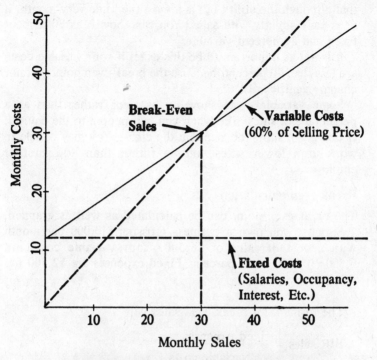

Figure 10-1/Break-Even Chart (in thousands of dollars)
B/E Sales Level of $30,000 per Month

point. Lower sales (to the left), will result in a loss; higher sales in a profit.

Fixed and variable costs

To determine the cost-sales curve, costs must be separated into those that are sales-dependent (variable costs) and those that stay the same (fixed or period costs). For most companies the "cost of sales" on the operating statement is a variable cost and the costs labeled "expenses" are fixed.

If your company's variable costs are more than 70 percent of sales it will be worth your while to be very precise about what is variable and what is fixed. For example, you may find that although the utility bill is almost the same very month, it does vary slightly with sales. You can show it as 80 percent fixed and 20 percent variable.

It is not as important to be this exact if your variable costs are less than 70 percent, because the break-even point will not change significantly.

Some variable costs show up as steps rather than as a percentage of sales, like when you add people to the payroll. If this is so, show the steps on the curve. You may decide to work at a lower sales volume rather than add another employee.

Break-even calculation

The break-even point can be calculated as well as graphed.

Suppose you own a business grossing $10,000 per month with a cost of sales of $6,500. Your variable costs are $6,500 \div 10,000$, or 65 percent. Fixed expenses are $2,500 per month.

The formula for break-even sales is:

$$\text{B/E sales} = \frac{\text{fixed expenses}}{1 - \dfrac{\text{variable costs}}{\text{sales}}}$$

So, in this case:

$$\text{B/E} = \frac{2,500}{1 - \dfrac{6,500}{10,000}} = \frac{2,500}{.35} = \$7,143 \text{ per month.}$$

Because $1 - \dfrac{\text{variable costs}}{\text{sales}} = \text{gross margin}$,

$$\text{B/E is also} = \frac{\text{fixed expenses}}{\text{gross margin}}$$

RATIO ANALYSIS

If you have monthly financial statements, keep a record of your backlog and your purchase commitments, and know

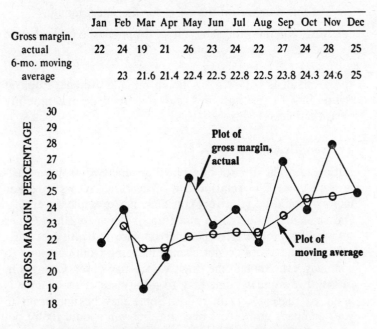

	Jan	Feb	Mar	Apr	May	Jun	Jul	Aug	Sep	Oct	Nov	Dec
Gross margin, actual	22	24	19	21	26	23	24	22	27	24	28	25
6-mo. moving average			23	21.6	21.4	22.4	22.5	22.8	22.5	23.8	24.3	24.6	25

Plot of gross margin, actual

Plot of moving average

Figure 10-2/Illustration of a "Moving Average"

your break-even point; then you have sufficient information to maintain control over your company's financial condition. I find that the quickest, easiest, and most useful way to do this is by ratios.

Ratios can be charted and compared with prior months. They can be compared with the ratios of other companies, regardless of size. Furthermore, so long as they are determined in a consistent manner, absolute accuracy is not important. It is the changes that are significant.

Smoothing

If a company normally experiences drastic variations from month to month, ratio charts will not be informative unless the monthly variations are *smoothed*.

Here is a technique for smoothing:

• Add the ratios for the last six months and divide by six. (Six-month average.)

- Put this number on the chart for the latest month.
- Next month do the same thing, dropping the earliest ratio and adding the latest one.

The result is called a six-month moving average. Look at figure 10-2 to see how this shows a trend despite monthly perturbations.

The significance of ratios

Ratios are indicators of interplay between two or more business factors. The relationship of certain factors to other factors should be relatively constant. For example, inventory and sales are expected to move up or down together. Other ratios, like productivity per person, are indicative of efficiency. The factors do not change meaning from company to company, even though the exact values may differ. Changes in ratios always mean something to a business. This chapter is going to suggest certain ratios. Some may be important to your company and others may not, but you should figure out which are which.

Earnings to sales

This is obvious ratio, usually expressed as a percentage. It tells you how successful your business is and also how volatile. Companies like supermarkets, which hover near 1 percent of sales, are extremely volatile. That means small changes in sales or costs can produce large swings in profits. Small businesses should keep pretax profits above 10 percent of sales in order to be good credit risks.

Another earnings ratio that is commonly used is ROI, or return on investment. This ratio is more significant regarding the value of the business.

Backlog to monthly break-even sales

This ratio tells you how much business you have at your lowest acceptable level of sales. If it drops close to your average delivery time, you are in trouble and must consider cutting back expenses quickly.

Backlog to average sales

This tells you how much work you have at present shipping levels. If it rises, you may consider expanding. If it falls, consider cutbacks or stretch-outs.

Inventory to backlog

Inventory should follow backlog. If this ratio rises, you are buying too much. If it falls, you may be in for shortages.

Cost of sales to inventory.

This is called *turnover*. If you use the cost of sales for an entire year, the turnover ratio should fall between 3 and 10, depending on the type of business you are in. High turnover means efficient use of cash. It may also indicate lost business as a result of failure to deliver.

Purchase commitments to backlog

This is similar to the inventory-backlog ratio but leads it in time. To reduce inventory you must cut back on purchase commitments, and vice versa. This ratio is extremely helpful when there are a number of persons authorizing purchases.

Output per employee

After a little while you will find the ratio value that is directly related to your break-even point. This is a ratio you want to be constantly increasing.

Current ratio

Current ratio is a figure of merit for liquidity that is used by financial people everywhere. It is the current assets divided by the current liabilities. The ratio should be 2 or higher, otherwise you have insufficient working capital.

Working capital

Working capital is not a ratio but is closely related to the current ratio. It is the difference between the current assets and the current liabilities, in dollars. This spread provides the financial capability for day-to-day operations.

Acid test ratio

Like the current ratio, this is a check for liquidity, but it is more severe. Add cash and accounts receivable, then divide by the current liabilities to determine the acid test ratio. The number should exceed one.

Accounts receivable to sales

This is your average collection time. If it rises, get tougher on your collections.

Gross margin

Sometimes called gross profit, this is usually expressed as a percentage. Gross margins vary from business to business and range from 15 percent to 50 percent. Insufficient gross margin means that prices are too low, costs too high, or competition too tough. If you cannot get a good gross margin you are in the wrong business.

Overhead rate

This is a ratio for bidding and for absorption of manufacturing expenses. Divide indirect manufacturing expenses by direct labor costs and express as a percentage. The number usually ranges from 75 percent to 150 percent. If the overhead rate goes up, it means that indirect and supervisory costs are becoming a greater part of the total costs. This may be a result of rising costs or of falling business levels. It is a danger signal because it affects today's profits and tomorrow's sales.

Equity to debt

This measures your company's borrowing ability. The ratio should be greater than 1 if you expect to borrow.

DIGGING DEEPER

You should be able to detect impending problems from the financial statements, but the chances are you will not be able to pinpoint the cause. For that you must dig deeper.

Overcontrol

If your business runs well without controls, leave well enough alone. Chances are, though, that it does need control. Most businesses do. Use your financial information to determine just what is needed. The least amount of control to keep your business running smoothly and profitably is what you should strive to obtain.

Homing in

Finding your difficulties is like playing the game "twenty questions." You separate the various possibilities into large chunks, eliminate the innocent, and carve the suspect into smaller portions. You do this by using numbers, not intuition.

Possibilities: sales or production?

There are only two major functions in your company, so decide between them. Is your loss of earnings caused by what is being sold, or by how it is being made? Answer this before you tear into the production manager.

You can tell this by examining your records. You will want to see if there have been changes in product mix, order size, delivery times, or customer mix. Any one of these things can affect profitability. You may find that product A, which normally made up 20 percent of your shipments, jumped to 40 percent in a month where profits were low. Product A becomes a prime suspect.

Digging this information out of your sales records will undoubtedly be a tedious and time-consuming job. On the other hand, keeping running records is a permanent expense. Don't start out with a lot of reports nobody will use. You will have enough of these when your company gets big. If you have to use the information on a regular basis then you should maintain ongoing records.

Cost information

Cost accounting is another large, complex field. Large companies have cost accounting department to keep track of different products and different jobs. In those companies, executives often err in taking the accounting information at face value.

The problem with cost accounting is that the accountants do not allocate indirect costs properly. In the conventional method of job costing, for example, a program using a lot of assembly help in a small area will be charged a much greater percentage of the rent than a program where a small number of people are assembling a very large system in a huge area.

Similarly, a large production program with trained personnel who require a minimum of supervision will be charged more for supervision than all the new, small programs that use up all of the supervisory time.

All this is true because accountants absorb overhead as a percentage of direct labor. Overhead expense is not caused by direct labor, however. It is caused by the number of events.

The cost of purchasing is created by the number of purchase orders required. The cost of production control is caused by the number of shop travelers written and followed. The cost of supervision is related more to the number of setups and the number of new people hired than it is to the number of people supervised.

In addition to being event-related, overhead costs are problem-related. In most companies, 20 percent of the jobs (or products) use up 70 percent of the overhead expenses.

How to get useful costs

If you want to do an effective job of cost analyzing, forget allocating costs and try to identify every cost as a direct cost. Figure out exactly how much supervisory time is spent on the product, how much executive time, and how much administrative time. Charge rent for the total floor space used. Identify advertising costs and telephone costs and accounting costs. If you have to guess, do so on the basis of what you think the costs are. Don't go by the way accountants say they are typically allocated. What you really are trying to determine is what your cost savings could be if you did not have the function you are analyzing. Then compare what you have found against the selling price of the service.

Job costs and product costs

Identifiable job or product costs are collected through the use of charge numbers. Employees enter the charge number of their activity on their time card. Purchase orders carry the charge number, which is later applied against the invoice. Materials transferred out of stores use a requisition with the charge number. All of these charges are collected and recorded against the inventory on that job. This can be done manually or by computer. Banks that handle payroll accounts will provide a payroll distribution report, showing dollars spent against each of the various charge numbers.

Process costs

When a product can have a large number of variations of standard processes, process costs are very helpful. A clothing factory may wish to know, for example, how much it costs for sleeves or for cuffs. Accurate process costs can be obtained by counting the number of pieces processed over a period of time and dividing by the costs of that department.

Use of cost data

- Identify profitable activities and less profitable ones.
- Provide control guide lines and quantify results for different functions and groups.
- Provide a basis for cost estimating and pricing.

Comparisons

When you get cost information, compare it with the budget or the original cost estimate. Find out the cause for any variations.

Localize the causes of excessive productions costs

If a production department cannot meet the cost budgets, there are many possible explanations. The estimate may have been too low. The design may have been too elaborate. The methods used for manufacturing may have been a poor choice. The procedures may be inefficient. The workers may have been unproductive. Or the cause may have been a lack of communications.

The latter instance is all too common. The engineering department designs the item without being informed of the targeted manufacturing costs. Or the engineering department releases its drawings piecemeal, so production never understands what the job is until it has been completed.

Finding the cause is a matter of persistence and judgment. The accounting figures will lead the way and will pinpoint the item that is the source of the loss, but you still have to find the reason behind it.

11
HOW TO PRICE

Pricing is a mish-mash of mathematical calculations, intelligence, intrigue, philosophy, intuition, and pure desperation. This categorizes it as an art rather than a science.

Whether you run a one-man store or a large factory, your objective is to price for maximum earnings within the constraints of your production capability and your conscience. You must juggle your information on costs with your judgment of what your customer will pay and how much he will buy. This act is perched on the unstable platform of competition.

There are two ways to approach pricing. One way is to start out with the price you would like to have and configure your business on the basis of that price. The other is to start out with costs and set prices to cover them. Either way, you must watch what the competition is doing.

METHODS OF PRICING

Pricing for maximum profits—the price-volume relationship

The price-volume curve is a business school concept. As a small businessman you will never see this in its pure form, but it is worth examining because there is always some relationship between price and sales.

FUEL SAVER, YEARLY ESTIMATE

Price	Sales	Revenue	Costs	Profit
per unit	(units)	(in thousands of dollars)		
$ 200	5,336	1,067	1,067	0
250	5,000	1,250	1,000	250
500	3,333	1,666	666	1,000
600	2,668	1,600	534	1,066
700	2,000	1,400	400	1,000
1,000	0	0	0	0

Figure 11-1 Fuel Saver, Yearly Estimate

In an unrestrained marketplace, the volume of goods bought varies inversely with price. A monopoly therefore sets its price to bring the greatest absolute profit.

Suppose you have developed a fuel saver that can reduce gasoline costs by 40 percent. Your cost to produce this item is $200. You determine that at $250 each you can sell 5,000 per month, and that at $1,000 you cannot sell any. If the relationship between the volume and the sales price can be determined, then the point of maximum return can be located. Figure 11-1 shows this, assuming a linear relationship. Maximum earnings are obtained at a price of $600 per unit. At $200 and at $1,000, the earnings are zero.

What you look for in real-life business situations is nonlinear relationships. For example, if you find that a small reduction in price will bring a large increase in volume, by all means lower the price. Conversely, if a large price increase has little effect on sales, the price should be raised.

Prices and buyer reaction

Market research firms have made mathematical models of the buying public. Your customers will not fit this model, however, because you undoubtedly sell to a small market segment. Your customers will probably act like people, and are therefore more or less unpredictable.

It has been shown that raising the price of certain supermarket products has resulted in increased sales. Maybe you have a similar situation in your store. Remember, one promotional inspiration is worth a thousand pricing formulas.

Gas stations face each other at all four corners of major intersections throughout the nation. Before there was such a thing as a gas shortage, the price-volume relationship was very specific. The lowest price of the intersection got all the business. Right after the Yom Kippur war, all a station needed to sell out its stock was an attendant on duty. Price did not mean anything.

Buyer's market

A *buyer's market* exists when the capacity to supply goods exceeds the demand. Typical examples: small radios and hand-held calculators. Cause: overdevelopment of the price-volume concept. Too many manufacturers trying to fill the same need. The major characteristic of a buyer's market is that futher price decreases do not increase the market size, although they may affect market share.

Seller's market

This is a condition of supply shortages, like the oil shortage in 1973. It has occurred in many different industries, particularly just after World War II. Increases in prices do not reduce market size. If you are like most of us, you will find that seller's markets are reserved for your suppliers.

Fixed-volume markets

If the U.S. government decided to build three new V.A. hospitals, that might establish the need for 2,000 beds. If so, that would be the market. No amount of price cutting would increase the number of beds purchased.

Because the U.S. government, particularly the Department of Defense, is the world's largest purchaser, there are many such fixed-volume requirements. If many companies are vying for the same business, the government's buyers will work the price down by pitting one supplier against another.

Markup pricing

Retail stores use markups to set prices. Pricing by markup is like working a break-even analysis backwards. Two numbers are required to determine the minimum markup: estimated sales and estimated expenses.

$$\text{Markup (min.)} = \frac{100 \times \text{expenses}}{\text{sales} - \text{expenses}} \text{percent}$$

Example:

Your analysis of the foot traffic indicates that your new store can gross $22,000 per month. You anticipate the following expenses:

your own salary	$1,500
2 clerks	1,400
bookkeeper (part time)	500
payroll-related expenses	600
rent	1,400
telephone	80
freight-in	100
delivery truck	170
your car	200
utilities	120
insurance	75
taxes and licenses	15
janitor service	140
misc.	70
TOTAL	$6,370

$$\text{Markup} = \frac{100 \times 6,370}{22,000 - 6,370} = 40\%$$

122

You will note that the markup is a percentage of the cost of goods sold, not of the sales price. This means you add 40 percent of the cost of the item to the cost to determine the selling price. An $80 item is marked up $32 and sold for $112. The gross margin, expressed as a percentage of sales, is 29 percent.

Use your intuition

You may decide (in the case above) that 40 percent markup is too high to be competitive. Okay, then try to get along with just one clerk. Or take slighly less for yourself. Then recompute the markup.

The importance of volume

You may say that a 40 percent markup is tolerable but working for a break-even is not. You did not start a business to make the same salary you could get elsewhere.

If you hold the 40 percent markup and can increase your sales level to $30,000 per month without increasing expenses, you will show a $3,200 monthly profit on top of your paltry salary. The alternative, raising the markup, might have resulted in lower sales. Those are the choices you must make.

Hang in there

Do not give away the store just to stay in business a little longer. Do not reduce prices in panic. Try to promote your products and your company. I had a business friend who always said, "If I go bellyup, it is going to be sitting on my hands—not working my butt off for some customer."

His business had the highest prices in the neighborhood and yet he managed to get his share of customers. Some of his competitors went broke trying to take business away from him.

Which comes first, higher volume or lower prices?

When you are starting out, make the high volume come first.

Pricing by cost estimates

Many businesses must provide firm price quotations even though the exact costs are not known. Much of the bid-and-award type of procurement is priced in this manner. Building contractors, system installers (air conditioning, public-address systems, closed-circuit TV, etc), and suppliers of custom machinery or electronics bid fixed prices on services even though they have never done exactly the same job before.

The prices are derived from cost estimates.

Because the environment is often that of extreme competition, there is always a tendency to be overly optimistic or to overlook certain costs. This can cost you dearly. A better practice is to prepare a conservative estimate and then make an arbitrary cut if the price appears to be too high.

Cost estimates should be prepared on standard forms that list all of the possible tasks encountered in your business. This ensures that none of the regular tasks will be forgotten in the heat of the bidding.

Cost estimates and absorption accounting

Most systems companies use the standard absorption accounting method when preparing cost estimates.

A typical bid from an electronic system contractor may look like this:

COST ESTIMATE

Materials and purchased parts	$ 1,500
Subcontracts	1,200
Direct Labor: 500 man-hours @ $6.00	3,000
Overhead: 100% applied to direct labor	3,000
Total, manufacturing costs	$ 8,700
G & A @ 20% manufacturing costs	1,740
Total costs	$10,440
Profit (15% of selling price)	1,842
Selling price	$12,282

This method of pricing is prescribed by government agencies. FAR form 1411 has a similar format for cost estimates that must be submitted with large bids.

To make such a bid you must know your overhead and G&A rates. If you are bidding to a government agency, you must be able to justify your quoted rates. If your accounting records have been maintained satisfactorily, your accountant will be able to figure the rates with ease.

Negotiated rates

If you are low bidder in a competitive award, neither the government nor a private company has any right to examine your books or your method of arriving at your bid. Often, however, winning an award is the start of a long series of price negotiations. The purchaser may imply that this is the way they do business and that future relations depend on your compliance. Try to hold firm and reject further price discussions if you know you are low-bidder.

Frequently contractors will hold negotiating sessions with two or more bidders in an attempt to get lower prices. If you get trapped in such a situation you will find that your overhead and G&A rates come under attack. Your expenses will be questioned. The buyer will tell you that he cannot "allow" certain costs to be considered. You may be confused by this convincing talk. If you have not lied to the customer you can stick with your price regardless of what he tells you, so long as the bid was a *firm, fixed price.*

If you are a sole source supplier, the government may have a right to a cost estimate from you and may be able to demand a lower price. In general, cost estimates can be refused unless the contract exceeds a rather substantial amount. Quite often the government is willing to accept other evidence that you are being fair with them, like prior quote histories or sales prices for similar devices to other customers. Whatever you do, do not lie in providing cost estimates or the buyer may have a claim against your company under the Truth in Negotiations Act.

If you have a *cost-reimbursement* type of contract from the government, allowable expenses are established by statute.

The government auditor will back certain costs such as interest out of your G&A expenses before establishing a rate. There is no way of fighting this, but make certain to read up on allowable expenses. (The contracting officer will show you his authority in the Federal Acquisition Regulations if you ask.)

Direct cost method of bidding

If you do not know your overhead rate or your G&A rate you can still bid on the basis of cost estimates using direct-cost accounting methods.

Example:

Company Y has total monthly expenses, exclusive of direct labor and direct material, of $40,000. It has 25 direct employees averaging 4,325 hours of work every month.

COST ESTIMATE

Direct labor: 6,000 man-hours at $6.00 an hour	$ 36,000
Direct material:	8,000
Other direct costs: (Consultants)	3,000
Total direct costs	$ 47,000

$$\text{Months worth of expenses allocable to contract} \quad \frac{6,000}{4,325} = 1.39$$

1.39 × $40,000 =	$ 52,000
Total costs	99,000
Profit	15,000
Selling price	$114,000

In a direct-cost approach, all expenses are considered period costs, expensed as incurred. Each contract must bear its portion of that cost. In the above example the expenses are borne on the basis of 100 percent capacity. If the company cannot be expected to run at 100 percent capacity, the allocated expenses must be increased. At 80 percent capacity the $52,000 figure would become

$$\frac{52,000}{.80} = \$65,000$$

To find the time equivalent, divide the contract man-hours by the average man-hours worked in a month. That will tell you how many months worth of expenses this contract must cover at 100 percent capacity.

Pricing by time and material

No matter how good your estimating abilities, you cannot make an accurate estimate if the task is undefined. For this reason activities like repair shops, plumbers, consulting firms, and research houses often charge on the basis of actual expenses. This type of pricing is called time and material or simply T & M. The risk of an improper estimate is borne by the buyer, not the seller.

The labor and the material provided are charged at a marked-up rate. From this markup the seller must pay his other expenses and product a profit. His only risk is setting a rate that is too low. The competition may be setting the rate that can be charged, but if not, here is a method for determining hourly labor charges.

Example for a repair shop:

Mechanics on payroll	(6)
Total weekly wages	$1,500
Other weekly expenses	$1,000
Total costs for week	$2,500
Profit	500
Desired revenue, week	$3,000

Hours available: total 6 × 40 = 240

Time spent on returns	15%
Idle time (breaks, etc.)	12%
Total	37%

Time available for customer service = 240 × .63 = 151 hours
Quoted hourly rate = 3,000 : 151 = $19.87

The above computation is based on paying mechanics for 40 hours of work every week and having the customer absorb all inefficiencies. In this case, the quoted charge works out to be more than three times the mechanic's wage rate.

Price averaging

Because of business peculiarities it is rarely possible to hold to exact markups or exact prices for all services. A system of price averaging is used so that the month-end results are the same as if they were used.

TV repairmen have a fixed price charge for repairing a set. That is because the cost of finding the trouble may dwarf the cost of repair. Could you see a TV repairman charging the owner of a $149 black-and-white set $200 for replacing a $2 transistor that took 40 hours to locate? He gets around that kind of problem by charging everyone $40 and hoping to make money at the end of the month. If the month-end revenues come up short, he raises the ante to $45. Some customers pay $45 for a $20 repair job and others get an $80 job for the same price.

The flat-rate book used by many automobile repair stations also is a form of price averaging. The customer pays the same for a fast mechanic as he does for a slow one.

In a retail establishment the owner sets different markups for different product lines. He does this on the basis of his feel for the market. At the end of the month he hopes to make his average markup.

The marketing input

Your salesman should have a voice in the pricing. He must make the guess as to what the customer is willing to pay. You must keep track of his performance in this respect. Most salesmen want prices that are unreasonably low.

Never let your salesmen get away with saying that your price is too high. He must say exactly how high. Working with a target price, you may be able to design a winning product.

Pricing and profit making

The best way to price is by what the item is worth to the user. If your product can save a company $10,000 every year, it certainly should be willing to spend $10,000 for the product, even if it cost you $2,500 to make. Your profit is not your customers' business. The value your service provides is. So, the best way to price is to price *benefits*.

Marginal costing

If your regular product line provides your company with sufficient margin to pay expenses, you may be able to increase profit by providing extra service at lower than normal markups. This is the concept of marginal costing or marginal pricing. When is this worthwhile?

- When your normal volume pays your expense.
- When the marginally costed item has high volume and can be used as a base for other business.
- When the product is an added feature, not computed in your operating plans.
- When the product can be squeezed into your present facilities at minor expense.

Examples of marginal costing

Restaurants normally price their fare at 2½ to 3 times the food cost. Desserts are exceptions because the diner can easily pass them up if the prices are too high.

Many appliance companies make private lines for large chains like Sears at reduced margins. These sales give them a base for absorbing expenses and help to level productivity.

Companies working to full capacity on the day shift can take long-term orders for night shift work if the price covers all the night shift costs and adds a little extra. It is not necessary to get paid a second time for the day shift expenses. Rent, executive salaries, equipment costs, and most of the selling expenses have been paid for.

Volume discounting

There are two justifications for volume discounting. The first is the lower direct costs resulting from improved efficiency and lower material costs. The other is the extra absorption of expenses associated with higher sales levels. Overabsorption of expenses is the greatest source of corporate profits. That is why volume discounts make sense.

The size of the discount depends on many things. If the order will require your full output or deplete your entire inventory, thereby depriving you of the opportunity to make normal markup sales, then the discount cannot be very large. If the order is over and above your normal sales, you can afford to give away a large share of its gross margin and still come out ahead. Make an expense forecast with and without the order. That will tell you how much you have to charge.

Pricing for market share

There is a theory that a company with a new product can maintain the major market share by methodically lowering prices and that the market will increase due to the price reduction and that the costs will decrease as a result of the larger volume.

There are examples where this phenomenon took place, but the theory depends upon too many ideal conditions. Texas Instruments seemed to be an adherent of this theory, and while it was successful for some semiconductors, it failed dismally on watches and home computers.

I strongly advise against pricing in accordance with any formula. Pricing is always a judgment matter.

Pricing to meet the competition

How low do you go to get an order? This is one dilemma that makes life as a small businessman less than ideal.

There is no hard-and-fast rule. If you are in a dogfight you are going to be hurt, no doubt about it. My inclination is to accept business down to the break-even point but no lower. This is not a hard-and-fast rule because you may be trying to bridge a particularly bad period.

If you can see a downturn in prices ahead of you, plot them on a graph and try to lower costs to match, even if this means cutting many frills. Prepare your sales department to fight harder for every order, large or small. Get your people thinking cost savings. Try to stay head of the business dip.

Judge the impact of your competitor's action. He may be capacity limited, in which case his lower price may not take that much business from you. In the aftermath of deregulation every airline in that suicidal industry reacted to every price cut regardless of the number of aircraft on any particular route. Pacific Express (now extinct) with one flight daily to Hawaii could throw United into a dither. Keep your head about you and do not panic. It is hard to reverse a price cut that is made prematurely.

Good pricing comes from knowledge and judgment

The more you know about your market and your company's financial status, the better you will be able to price, but there is no way to remove the element of judgment or to sideslip the finger of fate.

12
CONTROLLING
INVENTORY

When you save a dollar in inventory cost you get a seren-
dipitous reward: A lower inventory tax.

Inventory is an investment. Reducing inventory (or increasing turnover) raises the return on investment.

Inventory takes cash. Controlling inventory yields cash.

Inventory costs money just to have around. Stocking costs
range between 10 percent and 30 percent of the inventory
value. The national average is 25 percent.

But—inventory must be available when it is needed. You
cannot make sales without it.

So, strive for balance and control. You want inventory when
you need it but no more than necessary.

Sales forecasts

It is not possible to control inventory unless you have an idea
of how much you will be needing. This takes a sales forecast
by product.

Economic order quantity

Business texts concentrate heavily on economic order quantity (EOQ). This is the spot where total costs per unit are the
least. If you buy more than the EOQ, the storage costs rise

faster than the money saved through quantity discounts. Although the reasoning behind the EOQ theory is valid, I have never seen a small businessman use it, nor have I seen a place where its use was advisable. Too many facts must be accumulated to make a decent analysis. The circumstances are always changing. Cash considerations usually take precedence over price. Furthermore, when buyers can get a good price break they generally take it.

This is the last you will hear of EOQ from me.

OPEN TO BUY

Retailers often manage thousands of different items. Some are stock items with highly predictable sales levels. Sales of others cannot be forecast with any accuracy. Prices have wide ranges even in a single department. Quality and brands vary. Nevertheless, the well-being of the business requires that this inventory be controlled. To do so takes a *system* for authorizing purchase of replacement stock.

Establish priorities

Not every item can be controlled individually. There is not that much time in a day. The first step in any inventory control system is to recognize this fact and act accordingly.

Set priorities. Categorize inventory into that which will be controlled individually and that which will be controlled in bulk. Cost is the prime consideration but lead time also is important. Here are several methods for gross control.

Min-max

Set a minimum quantity and an order quantity based on the monthly sales and the lead time. For example, if you sell ten boxes a month and the lead time is three months, every time the supply gets down to forty, order another forty. (You could not afford this much inventory if the item were costly. The turnover is too low.)

Automatic ordering

Buy so many boxes a month. If you start running out, increase the order. If stock builds up, skip a month and reduce the order size. (You will lose a few sales because of lack of stock, but the inventory turnover will be much greater.)

Let the salesman do it for you

Ask the supplier's salesman to track your usage and hold the inventory to some preestablished amount. Check once in a while to see that he is not giving you the business.

Keep count

Keep a running count on all high-priced inventory. Your cardex file or computer print-out should show the opening inventory, the amount received, the amount sold, and a closing inventory for each month. Each item should be separate so that you can see no less than a year's activity at a glance. Figure 12-1 gives a sample.

Physical counts should be made frequently to verify the book records. A count should be made before any critical period, like Christmas. Discrepancies between book and physical count should be expected, but any consistent shortage is worth investigating.

Purchase of replacement stock should be made periodically, according to an open-to-buy formula. In addition, interim safety buys may be desirable when the stock hits a low point.

Open-to-buy formula

To keep sufficient inventory on hand for unexpected sales, but not so much as to waste cash, you must take into account such things as seasonal variations, random variations, anticipated sales, procurement lead time, order time, and desired turnover. A sample formula is given below, but whatever technique you use it must be seasoned with a little common sense. Adjustments must be made to fit the circumstances.

Sample formula

Snappy's Camera Shop expects to sell about 120 of its low-priced "instant" cameras every year. The selling price of this camera is $20 and its cost is $14. The owner wants to turn over the inventory at least 6 times, that is, he does not want more than $280 tied up in inventory for this camera.

He did not keep records last year and therefore cannot provide any seasonal adjustments. The lead time from the distributor is three weeks, so he expects to place a monthly order during the first week of every month for delivery on the first working day of the following month.

The total lead time, including order time, is one month. This is 10 units. Because the turnover allows an inventory of 20 units, the extra 10 provide a contingency for random variations.

The owner uses this formula for open to buy:

OTB = Controlled inventory level (20 units) + anticipated sales for the coming month − (inventory on hand + open orders).

Because anticipated sales are the same for each month, the formula becomes OTB = 30 − (inventory + open orders).

Figures 12-2 shows what could happen if sales were unexpectedly high (by 38 percent) and seasonal as well. Only 18 sales would be lost out of a possible 165. Inventory would turn over 23 times. If the owner had used a little common sense he would have bought a little extra when the stock dropped below 5, and would have eliminated those lost sales.

Figure 12-3 shows what would have happened if the owner had anticipated heavier sales during the warmer months but no increase in the total for the year. The heavier sales level would result in 12 lost sales instead of 18.

Had the owner guessed the correct amount for the year but applied no seasonal variation, the formula would have produced a turnover of 11 and only one lost sale. See figure 12-4.

Random variations

If variations are random they follow a Gaussian distribution curve and can be predicted mathematically.

Figure 12-1 Sample Inventory Record Card

DESCRIPTION _____ STOCK NO. _____

UNIT _____ LIST PRICE _____ COST _____ MAX. _____ MIN. _____

DATE	ORDER NO.	IN	OUT	BALANCE	UNIT COST	DATE	ORDER NO.	IN	OUT	BALANCE	UNIT COST

AICO-UTILITY Line Form No. 25-007

Figure 12-2/Snappy's Camera Shop/Inventory Record

	Jan	Feb	Mar	Apr	May	Jun	Jul	Aug	Sep	Oct	Nov	Dec	Total
Forecast sales	10	10	10	10	10	10	10	10	10	10	10	10	120
Sales possible	8	6	10	14	18	22	20	16	15	6	6	24	165
BOM inventory	20	12	16	14	6	0	0	0	0	1	9	18	
Units received	0	10	8	6	10	14	16	14	16	14	15	6	
Units sold	8	6	10	14	16	14	16	14	15	6	6	24	
EOM inventory	12	16	14	6	0	0	0	0	1	9	18	0	
OTB (units ordered)	10	8	6	10	14	16	14	16	14	15	6	6	
Lost sales	0	0	0	0	2	8	6	2	0	0	0	0	18

BOM = Beginning of month
EOM = End of month
OTB = Open to buy
Open to buy formula: OTB = 30 - EOM inv. + goods on order.

Figure 12-3/Snappy's Camera Shop/Inventory Record
Showing Seasonally Adjusted Sales Forecast

	Jan	Feb	Mar	Apr	May	Jun	Jul	Aug	Sep	Oct	Nov	Dec	Total
Forecast sales	6	6	6	14	14	14	14	14	14	6	6	6	120
Sales possible	8	6	10	14	18	22	20	16	15	6	6	24	165
BOM inventory	20	12	12	10	10	4	0	0	2	3	5	14	
Units received	0	6	8	14	10	14	16	18	16	8	15	6	
Units sold	8	6	10	14	18	18	16	16	15	5	6	20	
EOM inventory	12	12	10	10	4	0	0	2	3	5	14	0	
OTB	6	8	14	10	14	16	18	16	8	15	6	6	
Sales lost	0	0	0	0	0	4	4	0	0	0	0	4	12

OTB = 20 + anticipated sales for month - (EOM inventory + goods on order).

137

Figure 12-4/Snappy's Camera Shop/Inventory Record
Showing the Effect of a
More Accurate Sales Forecast Without Seasonal Adjustment

	Jan	Feb	Mar	Apr	May	Jun	Jul	Aug	Sep	Oct	Nov	Dec	Total
Forecast sales	14	14	14	14	14	14	14	14	14	14	14	14	168
Sales possible	8	6	10	14	18	22	20	16	15	6	6	24	165
BOM inventory	27	19	27	25	17	9	1	0	6	10	20	29	
Units received	0	14	8	6	10	14	18	22	19	16	15	6	
Units sold	8	6	10	14	18	22	19	16	15	6	6	24	
EOM Inventory	19	27	25	17	9	1	0	6	10	20	29	11	
OTB	14	8	6	10	14	18	22	19	16	15	6	6	
Sales lost	0	0	0	0	0	0	1	0	0	0	0	0	

OTB = 27 + 14 - (EOM inventory + goods on order).

A product that has average monthly sales of 10 will sell less than 5 or more than 15 only one month out of twenty.

For 20 to 1 odds that you will not miss a sale because of random variations, you should carry a safety stock equal to 1.6 times the square root of the expected sales.

Obviously, variations are casual as well as random. People buy more drugs during a flu epidemic.

Computerized inventory control?

Yes, a good computer system is worthwhile, but it is not a substitute for good judgment. It does not relieve the need for periodic counts. It must be checked for accuracy upon occasion. Just because a computer says a part is on hand does not mean that it is.

The worst part about a computerized inventory system is that it always follows the rules, and human intervention is difficult. People who use computers become enamored of them and less interested in the basic business objectives. When an exception to the rule is needed, it is less apt to be made with a computerized system than with a manual system.

If you are using a purchased program for inventory control, you have to work with it yourself to become familiar with its shortcomings. Do not assume you can turn it over to a clerk and forget inventory problems forever after.

MANUFACTURING INVENTORY

Guzintas

Retail businesses carry inventory for resale. Manufacturers use it as part of their own product: it guzinta (goes into) the end item. If nothing else, manufacturers buy raw material. They may also require components, subassemblies, and finished items. Companies selling to manufacturers are called OEM suppliers (original equipment manufacturers). The goods they sell are OEM items.

Buy-outs

Manufacturers of mobile homes and recreational vehicles often spend as much as 70 percent of their sales dollar on outside purchased parts. This is the high end of the range.

Electronic equipment manufacturers spend from 25 percent to 45 percent on buy-outs.

Machine shops, sheet metal fabricators, and other companies with high labor costs spend from 10 percent to 20 percent of sales on raw material purchases.

Regardless of how much is purchased, control is essential.

For the want of a nail

A twenty-cent part can hold up a month's shipment. Loss of the cash flow could be disastrous. A payroll could be missed.

Little parts assemble into bigger parts. High-level assemblies cannot be started until lower-level items are completed. So nothing can be left to chance.

Inventory control in a manufacturing environment

As in a retail establishment, absolute control over everything is impossible. This applies to large companies as well as small. Priorties must be established and inventory categorized.

The following story about a manufacturer of electronic and microwave instruments illustrates how inventory management can be improved.

The problem

Farought Instrument Corp. grew from $2 million annual sales to $3 million in a little more than one year, but the increased production level seemed to be more than it could handle.

Most of the instruments were sitting in finished-goods stores waiting for a missing part so that they could be completed and tested. Customers were livid. Phone lines were buzzing all day with buyers demanding overdue items.

The purchasing department had three full-time expediters and two material control planners trying to straighten out the mess but the task seemed overwhelming. There were just too many parts to track.

In desperation, the president hired a consultant, who made the following analysis:

The company had shipped $3,030,000 worth of instruments during the past twelve months. New orders had fallen recently because of stretched-out delivery times.

Materials and outside purchased parts in the shipments had cost $1,100,000 (36 percent).

The average monthly inventory as shown on the balance sheets was $450,000, of which $180,000 was work in process and finished goods. Raw material and purchased parts accounted for $270,000.

Almost 60 percent of the company's sales were of a single product, a $1,250 instrument. An analysis of the bill of material for this instrument showed that purchased parts and material cost $430 per unit. This was 34.4 percent of the selling price.

There were 286 items in the instrument. Several different groupings by price were attempted, and this one was found to be the most revealing:

35 items cost more than $5 each. The total was $290. The highest price was $27, the lowest was $5.

There were 74 items that cost at least $1 but less than $5 each. ($112 in all.)

The remaining 177 items, costing under $1 each, accounted for $28.

Recapping: 12% of the items cost 67% of the total.
26% of the items cost 26% of the total.
62% of the items cost 7% of the total.

Other instruments showed a smiliar spread in parts value.

The solution

Inventory was categorized into groups A, B, and C.

Group A had a total of 60 items accounting for about $700,000 of annual procurement. These items were followed constantly by two of the expediters and one planner. Advanced deliveries were cut back. The average inventory of these parts was reduced from $180,000 to $94,000 because of the added supervision.

Group B inventory was ordered on a monthly basis according to the sales forecast. Of the items in Group B, only 19 had lead times of over one month. $14,000 was spent for safety stock on those 19 items. The material control planner was given authorization to buy up to one month's supply of any item that appeared to be at a dangerously low inventory level.

Group C inventory was put on a min-max basis. Approximately $20,000 was ordered for immediate purchase, bringing in a six-month supply. Engineering was asked to use the same items on new designs wherever possible.

In six months the company was about 90 percent on schedule, up from 34 percent. Material shortages were rare and only one had been serious. Shipments were over $300,000 a month (up from $250,000), but the inventory had dropped from $450,000 to $410,000. Although over 20 people had been added to assembly and test departments, no additions had been made to the overhead personnel. The overhead rate had dropped 12 percent.

Inventory stocking and recording

Manufacturing companies keep two types of stock, general stock and job stock. The general stock is bought for use on all jobs. When requisitioned to a particular job it becomes job stock. Parts can be purchased also directly into job stock.

Job stock can be maintained in bins with other similar parts or can be assembled into "kits." Kits are "pulled" against next assemblies. All the parts going into the next-highest assembly are collected in one box for transfer to the production department when called for.

Missing parts required to complete a kit are called shortages. The sooner a kit is pulled, the earlier shortages come to light, so pull kits well in advance of need and make up a shortage list. Get the expediters working to clear the shortages.

Buying

In a retail store the buyer is a key employee. He does more than place the purchase order. He anticipates the needs. This is *the* knowledge-job in a retail store.

Price is only one of many factors the buyer uses in placing orders. More important than price is whether the product fits the store's image. Competitive bidding is used at times, but the final purchase decision is usually a value judgment.

In a manufacturing company the buyer is more an administrator than a creator. He buys what others have specified. To the extent that he selects the right vendors, controls their response, and follows up on delivery, he performs a valuable service. He must also know enough about the product he is procuring to decide when to buy on price and when to buy on value.

In the manufacturing environment, competitive bidding is the general practice. Buyers often play one vendor against another to get lower prices. Preferred suppliers are sometimes given "last look," that is, they are told what price will take the order.

Small companies must buy from dependable suppliers. The price need not be the lowest nor the quality the best, but the quality must be exactly as represented. Chasing unreliable vendors, trying to get them to make good on their promises, is too time consuming for the small businessman.

Just-in-time procurement

This is a Japanese innovation taking hold at some U.S. manufacturers. It is an attempt to eliminate storage and all purchased-part inventory. The purchased item goes from the carrier's truck to the factory floor. You had better know exactly what this entails before you try it.

13

GETTING IT DONE

If you have experienced nothing but broken promises, late deliveries, and substandard quality in your personal and business life during the past few years, you may think that a good job is one that was completed years ago. That is not true.

Every day you are a witness to some of the most complicated jobs of scheduling and planning, involving diverse talents and innovative technologies that must be welded into a contiguous whole with flawless timing. These tasks are executed so skillfully that you take them for granted. You may even criticize them for failing to achieve absolute perfection. Of course I am referring to television programming.

Few jobs require so much skill or meeting such demanding schedules, yet there is almost never a delay, and if there is a failure it is from an artistic, never the production, standpoint.

This is so because the people responsible know that failing to meet a deadline is unthinkable.

The same people, when making a movie for theater presentation, may end up a month late on a three-week shooting schedule.

Aerospace companies, known for their sloppy work habits and schedule performance, almost always are on time with the space shot that has a narrow launch window.

Doing a good job is 10 percent planning and 90 percent attitude. The TV programmers and space shot suppliers were driven by a sense of urgency. It is a powerful motivator.

Unfortunately, you cannot instill a sense of urgency when the facts are not supportive. It has been tried but it rarely works. Few people will apply your standards of urgency or importance to their efforts. If you have a real emergency, let them know about it and they will respond. Do not expect them to be stirred by word pictures of corporate profits.

Build pride

This was a subject of chapter 7, but it is covered here in the narrower aspect of building productivity. Groups that have a widespread reputation for doing a good job try to live up to that reputation. Kelly Johnson's "Skunk Works" at Lockheed was renowned for its productivity even though most of Lockheed suffered from a reputation for the opposite.

Within many large companies there are "tiger teams" of elite personnel who revel in polishing off the toughest jobs.

It depends on you

Pride starts with your attitude. You must show people that you want a quality product, on time. You can make a point of praising and rewarding those people who are competent and productive.

If you take no apparent interest and, worse, if you reward those who are unproductive or disruptive, company morale will deteriorate quickly. As the man in charge it is your job to recognize the people who contribute and to separate them from those who do not. This is not an easy task. You must master it, however, for your company will not operate smoothly unless you do.

Cut through the smoke screens

It is not how hard an employee works or how many hours he puts in. It is what he accomplishes. Everyone in your company is trying to convince you that he is doing an outstanding job. Employees will point out their loyalty or their style or their sacrifices. But many of them are phonies (although perhaps unaware they are phonies).

If you can recognize which ones are the phonies your employees will applaud your insight and work all the harder. If you latch onto the glitter and ignore the gold, your employees will sink into despair. They want to see the good guys win.

Make it easy to get things done

Many of the obstacles to doing a good job are placed there by management for its own convenience. Management convenience is not a corporate necessity. It is the workers' jobs that should be made easier. Managers should remove obstacles. That is an important part of their jobs.

Insist on quality

The quality of your product depends upon your interest. If you are not out on the floor looking at the product and talking to the workers about its quality, you simply will not get quality. If you put profits ahead of quality, you will not get quality and later you will not get profits either. If you don't care what your customer is getting, there is no way you can make your employees care. You are better off working for someone else. If you do care, show it and insist upon it.

In every case where the Japanese eroded the American market position, lack of quality allowed them to squeeze into the marketplace. The Japanese make quality products because their managers place quality foremost. Once entrenched, they are almost impossible to displace because of quality.

In this mad world of cut-rate air transportation, Singapore Airlines always goes out with high-load factors at full fares. People want to experience their service. Your reputation for quality can get you through some bad times, too.

Insist on performance

Accept no excuses for missed schedules, poor quality, or excessive expenditures. Let no one be misled about your displeasure. Management limits performance if it expects anything less than the best.

146

Philip Crosby based his "zero defects" program on this very premise and was able to achieve quality records that surpassed all expectations.

Make performance obvious

Schedules and status should be drawn on big charts and posted near the production lines. Monthly output results should be hung over the work tables where the finished items are placed for inspection. You should be able to walk through the manufacturing department any day of the month and tell how everything is going without asking a question.

Visit the factory often

It is surprising how many company presidents do not know what is going on in their factories. Your presence helps. It tells people you think their job is important. Chat with the workers at break time. Tell them what is happening. They will spread the word. Listen to what they have to say. They know more than any of your managers about what is going on.

Warning: *Treat what you hear with caution. If supervisors find they are hurt by the workers' tidbits, they will put the screws on. Use with finesse the information you glean.*

Keep the factory clean and uncluttered

People work harder in a clean area and when they think they are being watched.

The factory manager should be able to see from one end of the plant to the other, so use low-profile bins, work benches, and equipment wherever possible. The factory manager's office should have a glass window facing the production area.

Give people time to clean house before leaving, and make sure they use that time.

Plan all jobs

The manufacturing department must plan its work to match the company's overall plans. Maintaining control over the basic manufacturing processes is an extremely important factor in producing profits. Important planning tools are the shop-load schedule, the machine-load schedule, and the traveler or job ticket.

Shop loading

Shop loading is done by plotting available personnel against job backlog so that each job is started on time. The key word is *start*. Jobs should be scheduled by start and end times, not by completion date. A job that is not started on time will not be done on time. Figure 13-1 shows a simple but effective shop-load chart.

Machine loading

Just as you can get only so much out of your people, you can get only so much out of your machines. A machine-load chart looks like the shop-load chart except that machine numbers replace workers' names.

Your machine loading should tell you when a night crew is advisable or show you which machine you can sell. It may even convince you to buy another engine lathe or paint booth.

Travelers

The traveler is a ticket that stays with the job from start to finish. It lists all of the operations in chronological sequence. It may or may not have dates, depending upon the leeway allowed the individual foremen in establishing their own work loads.

Who makes the plans?

This depends on your company setup. It can be the production manager, the production control planner, the process engineer, the foremen, or even you. Plans are only half the battle. The other half is follow-up. Make certain someone has that responsibility also.

Use foremen extensively

Make your foremen managers as well as pushers. Get them looking upstream for the tools of their next job. Have them

Figure 13-1/Shop-Loading Chart

	Employee									
Job Order #	Start	Compl	Start	Compl	Start	Compl	Start	Compl	Start	Compl

check engineering drawings and availability of parts *before* the job hits their station.

Give them a chance to raise hell with the engineers and buyers. Nobody knows any more about what it takes to get the job done than the foreman in charge, so give him a say about how the company is run.

Funnel all work through the foreman

Do not allow engineers, planners, or expeditors to tell workers what to do without going through the foreman first. Do not do it yourself. So far as the worker is concerned, the *foreman* should be the company.

Basic rules of behavior are more important than systems

Your people will make your plant go if they want to, if they know what to do, and if you do not stand in their way. If your people won't do it, nothing will.

14

WHOM DO YOU TRUST?

Nowadays only a small percentage of nonretail businesses can operate on a cash basis. Even many retail stores offer credit. Losses due to bad accounts can be very serious. It is not unusual that a company fails because of unpaid debts.

If your credit losses are running more than 0.5 percent of sales they are too high. There are two things you can do to reduce them: institute a tougher credit policy and reduce the allowable credit limits

Approving credit

Credit applicants should be screened for the three "C"s: character, capacity, and capital. The applicant should have a record of paying bills promptly, the means to make payment, and capital that can be relied on in case of emergencies.

Information sources

Every city has one or more mercantile credit agencies that can be retained for credit-checking purposes. Most of these agencies have computerized information banks, so they have up-to-date knowledge of recent transactions. They do not have good information about the financial status of the credit applicant, however.

National credit agencies like Dun and Bradstreet keep tab on financial condition as well as payment records. If the company reported on is public, the information will be taken from SEC reports and will be relatively up to date. Privately held companies are able to conceal adverse information, however, so these credit agencies are not foolproof.

Credit men often exchange information, so you can build up a list of people in other companies and check with them before issuing credit.

Salesmen are an excellent source of enlightenment about customer well-being. They can pick up tidbits from other salesmen, check the number of cars in the parking lot, and question company employees about the way business is going.

Get financial statements from all credit applicants. Watch out for "notes due" on the balance sheet, because they may be window dressing. The notes may be from owners or from sources with no capital.

Get personal guarantees

If a privately held company wishes an open account from you, have the account personally guaranteed by the president and even one of the vice-presidents. Do not be bashful about asking. If they have any hesitancy about complying you can view it as a warning. Obviously, if the company has a large, easily verified line of bank credit, this request for personal guarantee would be inappropriate.

Set credit limits

The credit limits you set must be based on what you can afford to lose and on what you think the applicant can afford to carry. The limits should be set both in amount and in time of payment.

Credit is a cash drain

When you give credit you deprive yourself of cash. So, you must either have sufficient cash to run the business in spite of the credit or you must borrow to make up the difference.

Credit is an expense

Unless you charge interest on open accounts (a rare situation) you will have a real cost equal to the credit you have extended times some applicable interest rate. This is true whether or not you have borrowed money.

There is the additional expense of credit checks, bookkeeping, and bad accounts.

You must follow up

Do not let your customers get into the habit of paying 30-day terms in 45 days. Get on the telephone and insist on payment. You will not lose customers by asking for your money when it is due.

Something to remember: *The key to debt collection is to never let a debt get old.*

Formalize your credit policy

Write down the conditions required for the granting of credit and the conditions required for the maintaining of credit. Be very careful about making any exceptions.

Important: *Centralize credit granting in one person only. If that person is not you, do not circumvent him.*

Collections

If you have bad accounts, pursue them diligently. If you do not have the stomach for bill collecting, find someone in your company who does. Use the gradual approach: first a "friendly reminder," then a demand for immediate payment, and finally legal action. If the unpaid account is large, you will want to hire an attorney. Otherwise it can be turned over to a collection agency.

If the bill gets to the point where you must enforce collection you will lose anywhere from one-third to one-half of the amount in collection costs. For this reason it may be better for you to work out pay-down terms with the debtor. You are much better off getting full payment over a year than going through litigation.

On the other hand, if the debtor is close to liquidation, you should get whatever you can as quickly as you can.

The best way to set your course of action is to visit with the defaulter and learn as much as you can about the company and the people in it.

If you are dealing with an individual, the same principle holds. Given a little breathing room, he may repay all of the debt or he may take advantage of you. You have to size him up and make your decision.

Getting the runaround

Your slow accounts are in all likelihood slow with all of their suppliers. Under the gun they have learned how to get a few more days of credit. Of course, we have all heard one of the three big lies, "The check is in the mail." How about when you get the check and it is not signed? Do you think this is just an honest mistake?

Companies have been known to have bank accounts across the country and to pay with a check drawn on the farthest bank, just for the extra few days of float. A strong magnet can be used to demagnetize the numbers on the bottom of a check. This delays payment about a week, since the rejected check must be processed by hand. Checks which bounce are common, and there is always a plausible excuse, "Oh, we changed banks and a few checks got caught in the process." How about checks which have one number in figures and an entirely different amount written out? A mistake? Hardly, but what can you say? Watch for signs of the runaround and tighten up. Remember the best time to get your money is when you have something they need.

Stop shipments

When an account becomes overdue be certain that all additional shipments are put on hold. The units you hold back may be the leverage you require to extract payment. If the product is unique you will still not lose anything, because the customer has breached the contract by failing to make payment. If there is more than one contract in existence then you cannot simply hold up shipment on contracts where no money is due.

First, you must make a written demand for adequate assurance of performance (suspending your own performance while waiting a reasonable time for a reply). If no reply is received send written notice that you regard the contract as having been repudiated.

The good customer dilemma

During the credit crunch of the late seventies and early eighties, many suppliers were faced with very slow payments from their best customers, some of whom were large multinational corporations. They had the choice of cutting off these big accounts or of getting further behind on collections. In many cases the small suppliers lost their businesses following different credit policies. It was a case of being damned-if-you-do and damned-if-you-don't. The safer course is to stop giving credit quickly and to insist on payment. This is not easy, since big company finance departments become amazingly inacessible when they are falling behind in payments. If you have a large account which means much to you, take precautionary steps before the storm clouds appear. Get to know the comptroller of the company. Invite him to dinner occasionally just as you might the purchasing manager. Discuss business at dinner so that you can get a feel for the financial condition of the company (or division). Make yourself a friend who can help you later on.

Sometimes it works to your advantage to be tough on payments. Customers often feel embarrassed to go back to people they have hurt. When times get better they feel more comfortable with suppliers who have paid in a reasonable time.

BANKRUPTCY

The term "bankruptcy" means a state of commercial failure or an inability to pay debts. However, when we say a company is bankrupt we more than likely mean that it has been adjudged bankrupt by a bankruptcy court under the federal bankruptcy laws.

Bankruptcy Acts

Bankruptcy comes under federal jurisdiction and is governed by the Bankruptcy Acts. A person or corporation may petition the courts for protection under the bankruptcy laws or he may be forced into bankruptcy by creditors.

The bankruptcy laws serve two purposes:

- They free the debtor from further harassment by creditors after he has given up the assets he possesses, thus permitting him to rehabilitate himself and start life anew.

- They assure fair treatment to all creditors and protect the assets of the bankrupt on behalf of the creditors.

Straight bankruptcy

Chapters I through VII of the Bankruptcy Act apply to straight bankruptcy, which means termination of the business and liquidation of all assets for distribution to the creditors.

Chapter XI

When a company believes it has a chance of maintaining a viable business if only it could be relieved of some of its debts, it may file under Chapter XI of the bankruptcy laws.

The debtor is allowed to continue in business while he attempts to formulate a plan of rearrangement that is acceptable to a majority of the creditors, both in number and in amount. If he succeeds and the plan is approved by the court as being fair and equitable, the company may be discharged from bankruptcy and continue in business. No creditor can make a claim against the company for any more than the agreed-on amount, unless there was fraud involved or unless the creditor had not been notified of the bankruptcy hearings.

A trustee will be appointed by the court to represent the creditors and to collect funds due them. A receiver may or may not be appointed to run the business while the arrangement is being formulated.

Types of settlements

When a company files under Chapter XI there are usually few assets for the payment of unsecured debts. Such collateral as accounts receivable and inventory probably will have been pledged to some commercial credit company or bank. Fixed assets are likely secured against the purchase agreement. Liquidation would mean a few cents on the dollar for the average creditor. Because of this, settlements of 10 to 20 percent, in cash, are common. Longer-term settlements in the form of notes or preferred stock may be more generous. Very few companies surviving Chapter XI are able to continue for long without outside support, so the smaller amount in cash is often the best choice for creditors.

Chapter X

The only other portion of the bankruptcy laws of concern to small businessmen is a Chapter X reorganization. This is very similar to Chapter XI except that it can bring stockholders and other equity holders under the court's jurisdiction. Chapter X reorganization is a more likely form of bankruptcy for a large corporation with diverse types of issued securities. The results of a Chapter X also are likely to be the same: a very small recovery for the unsecured creditors.

Voluntary bankruptcy

Any person or any business can file a petition for protection under the bankruptcy laws. There are no prerequisites. The company may be solvent but wish to protect itself against some potential judgment.

When a company is, in fact, insolvent or unable to pay its debts as they come due, it may seek refuge under the bankruptcy laws while going after additional capital or finding a corporate buyer.

Involuntary bankruptcy

If it seems that a person or a business is trying to defraud creditors or treat one creditor better than others, a bankruptcy may be forced by a group of three or more creditors.

The creditors must be able to prove that the debtor committed one or more of the following acts:

- Transferring property with intent to delay or defraud creditors.
- Making a preferential payment to one creditor when insolvent.
- Permitting, while insolvent, a lien on property that has not been discharged within 30 days.
- Making a general assignment for the benefit of creditors.
- Permitting the appointment of a receiver.
- Admitting, in writing, an inabiity to pay debts and a willingness to be adjudged bankrupt.

Desirability of forcing bankruptcy

As a creditor, you want to keep your debtor out of bankruptcy. It usually takes a long time, perhaps years, between the first sign of financial weakness and bankruptcy. If you can detect the signs, act to cut off further credit and collect your debts.

If there is any fraudulent attempt to deprive you of payment, get to your attorney quickly. If not, pursue your own claims diligently but do not join with others in forcing bankruptcy.

15

HOW TO HANDLE
LAWYERS
AND ACCOUNTANTS

The easiest way to get a spirited conversation going at any businessmen's meeting is to start talking about lawyers or accountants. Dissatisfaction with or frustration by those two professional groups has created a common bond between businessmen everywhere.

It is unfortunate, because accountants and attorneys are essential to business and, properly used, can make key members of any management team.

Of course, the criticism is not completely undeserved. Lawyers and accountants share many characteristics. For one, they think it is harder to be a member of their profession than to be a good businessman. Moreover, most of them think that they are good businessmen whether or not they have any business background.

Lawyers and accountants are not natural material for the making of businessmen. They have been trained differently.

Lawyers are conditioned to keep clients out of trouble, to avoid risks.

Accountants are disciplined to rely upon numbers and to reject intuition and value judgments.

A businessman is by nature a risk taker who will often fly by the seat of his pants. Professional experts should be there to help the business leader evaluate the risks, not to scare him away.

Using professional help effectively

When you are in litigation the attorney is the team captain. Until that time, you are. Professional experts are members of the management team. Their inputs are to be weighed like any other inputs. And questioned, too, because it is always possible that they are wrong.

The professional opinion must be separated from any business advice. You should be told the legal implications of your actions, the possible consequences and the measure of risk. That is a legal input of business value.

Or you should be told the accounting alternatives with their resultant ambiguities or inaccuracies. That is an accounting input to a business decision.

Having asked a professional opinion you may then solicit business advice. Do not accept stereotyped phrases like, "Everybody loses when you go into litigation." I have heard that statement many times, but it is obviously not always true.

Lawyers

Attorneys are naturally very cautious. They do not want to be on the losing side in any litigation. This hurts their firm's reputation. You must make those major decisions.

I have recently seen a law suit successfully pursued against the advice of the company's counsel. He knew too much about the case and felt the legal position was weak.

The outside attorney who was hired as a trial lawyer had no such trepidations. He built a solid case from the disclosure proceedings and won a significant judgment.

Most contracts are ambiguous. When legitimate claims are pursued the result is likely to be a compromise. If your legal position is weak and your lawyer reluctant to pursue the matter, do not give up. Have a layman who knows nothing about the law try to get a compromise. If you have a claim based on fairness or equity you will be surprised how well he can do.

Be careful when an attorney says he will check something out in advance. He may be applying for an advanced ruling from some government agency. You do not want an advanced ruling unless you can afford to take no as an answer.

Keep your attorney informed about what your business plans are. Soon he will get a feel for the way you operate and will become a valuable team member. Like any other employee, if he has faith in you he will do a better job for you.

When an attorney is essential

- When the other party has contacted you through its attorney.
- When dealing with corporate securities other than very simple private placements.
- When a union starts organizing your plant.
- When you want to fight the IRS.
- To apply for patents, copyrights, and trademarks.
- To make large purchases or sales outside normal business activities, like acquisitions, real estate, etc.

When to avoid lawyers

With lawyers pouring out of law schools at record rates and fees rising in spite of the excess supply, it is important for a businessman to keep the attorneys out of his day-to-day business. So that is my most important message. If the law affects your normal business operations, you learn it. You do not have to go through four years of law school to become familiar with a narrow body of laws. Here are other instances where it is best to avoid attorneys:

- When the amount in dispute is under $10,000, and there is no confusion about the law.
- Settling terms and conditions related to a sale of your company's product or the purchase of business supplies.
- Negotiating a deal—any deal. Make what you negotiate subject to an attorney's review, but keep lawyers out of the negotiation process.

• Dealing with government employees who are not lawyers.

Fees

Busy lawyers charge high fees. As a result, hiring one for minor disputes is not economical. You have to find an alternative, like settling between principals, going to small claims court, or becoming your own attorney. Even if you can find a lawyer willing to take your claim on a contingency basis, you have to realize that the time he spends must be limited. Yet the amount of time needed is often independent of the dollars at risk.

Other jobs, like starting a new corporation, are done often enough that they become a fill-in task on the word processor for the secretary. These are usually reasonably priced.

If you really need an attorney, you should get a good one. You can't give this job to the low bidder. Rather than bargain about hourly rate, discuss those things you or your employees can do to reduce his work load.

Fee gouging

Fee gouging and building up of unnecessary costs are not unknown phenomena. The asbestos claims against John Manfield and other companies is a prime example of how attorneys will ride a gravy train once their clients are locked onboard. I have personal knowledge of a law firm which withheld knowledge of a settlement offer from its client, fought, and lost a month-long court battle instead. The client not only paid more for the judgment but had to ante up $80,000 more for the lawyers. At least he rejected the advice of the attorney about appealing.

If you think you are getting the business, change lawyers if you can.

Accountants

Your certified public accountant has been licensed by the state. His income depends upon that license, so you cannot expect him to bend rules to suit your ends.

When a CPA audits your books he will render an opinion that will become part of your audited financial statement.

The financial statement is the company's statement. The opinion belongs to the accountant. For your company to obtain an unqualified opinion, the statement, including all of the footnotes, must comply with accepted accounting practices and your auditor must have satisfied himself as to the overall accuracy of the numbers.

If your corporation is closely held and you intend to keep it that way, your audited statement will be used primarily by prospective creditors. If the statement has some auditing qualifications the lender will make appropriate adjustments and may still proceed with the loan.

On the other hand, if you intend to go public you must have three years of audited financial statements. Any qualification would have to be removed before a reputable underwriter would accept your business.

Finding lawyers and accountants

The best source of information about professional help is the other businessmen you know. The closer their business resembles yours, the more weight you should place on their recommendation.

Suggestions from other sources, like banks and the bar association, will not be very reliable but your accountant may be able to recommend a good attorney, and vice versa.

Interview

When you find a likely candidate, interview him as you would a prospective employee.

- Find out about his specialties.

- Get the names of associates he uses for areas outside his expertise, like tax law or securities law.

- Ask about clients in businesses similar to yours. Let him tell you what he has done for them.

- Get his billing rates. Ask if he bills at the same rate for his secretary's time.

- Find out how long he has been in practice and estimate how well he has been doing.

Making a choice

When you put all the factors together and make a decision, do not be too disappointed if it is the wrong one. There is no way of telling how well he will blend with your company until you have been together for a while. If he does not work out, make a change. There should be no reluctance on your part. Unfortunately, many businessmen are hesitant about changing professional agents because they feel they are attacking their competence.

Increase your knowledge

The man who said war was too serious to leave to the military might have extended that comment to lawyers and accountants. If you want to be able to evaluate your expert help you must know something about their fields. The more you learn about accounting and business law the better you will call your shots.

The reverse also is true

The more your accountant and lawyer know about your business the better they will serve it.

Dos and don'ts about dealing with attorneys

- Make your lawyer part of the management team. Let him participate in basic business decisions.

- Question him. Get him to show you the law if you have any doubts.

- Differentiate between what you are entitled to legally and what you can negotiate.

- Give your attorney firm dates for responses and hold him accountable.

- Do not let your attorney reopen a deal that has already been made. It is the quickest way to throw away a lot of hard work.

- Do not let your attorney check things out in advance with government agencies unless you are prepared to accept a no or a maybe.

- Do not let your attorney handle nonlegal work or have extensive dealings with nonattorneys in other organizations.

- Conversely, do not let nonattorneys in your organization deal with outside attorneys on their own.

- When your attorney says you cannot do something, ask him what would happen if you did it anyway.

- If you have to negotiate from weakness, send a layman. He will probably make a good compromise and apologize for not doing better.

- If your attorney tells you, "You hired me for my advice, and if you do not follow my advice you should get another attorney," get another attorney. Whether or not you follow advice is your decision.

Dos and don'ts about accounting

- Install an accounting system that suits your needs. If your accountant finds fault with it, get him to change it without eliminating the features you want.

- Be leery about systems that are incorporated to simplify accounting. Remember, the systems that pay off are those that make life easy for those who sell and make products.

- Do not publish reports that nobody uses or install procedures that people cannot understand.

- To simplify your year-end audit and hold costs down, have your own accountant do the reconciliations and trial balances in advance of the audit.

- If you are dissatisfied with some audit decision, appeal it to the partner-in-charge.

- Tell your employees to answer all auditors' questions but volunteer nothing and, above all, make no facetious comments.

- Get the CPA to survey your control systems while he is making the audit. This is a most valuable accounting service. You should have checks and balances on all finances.

CPAs and management frustration

If you ever expected that business would be one endless sequence of rewarding personal accomplishments, your first audit will wash away such illusions.

You will find that many of the things you have done were for nought as far as the profits for the year are concerned. Even though they made business sense, they had no standing under approved accounting practices.

Junior accountants, who seem to be everywhere, spend most of the time asking obvious questions and educating themselves about your business. If you wonder who is paying for their education, your doubts will be dispelled quickly by the audit manager. You are, but at a reduced rate (slightly above your own salary).

You may also get the impression that each junior accountant is a budding Sherlock Holmes, anxious to uncover the latest Equity Funding scandal that he knows lies somewhere in that jungle of ledgers and journals. He will double-check everything, including the wastebaskets, for hidden clues. In spite of this, you know that any one of *your* machinists could steal your latest Bridgeport out from under his nose.

The best part of the audit is reading, on the bill, the explanation of why the charge exceeds the original estimate.

Once the experience is over and you have had a chance to return to normal you may wonder if they are all like that. Relax. You only have to put up with it once a year.

Can I give you any advice on how to make an audit less painful? Yes, turn it over to a subordinate and get out of town.

RECAPPING THE CHAPTER

Remember, it is you who is responsible for the running of your business, not your accountant or your attorney. It is more important to get them to answer your questions than it is to listen to their advice. Once you understand your options, you can make an intelligent business decision.

16

HOW TO SURVIVE IN SPITE
OF CONTRACT LAW

Articles I read during the preparation of this chapter were quite scary about contractual matters and universally recommended liberal use of attorneys. The trouble is that the articles were all prepared by attorneys.

A psychiatrist, sampling the world population through his patients, might assume that all people have some mental derangement. I have even read articles to that effect. Similarly, lawyers might have a slanted viewpoint. They may believe that every sloppily drawn contract results in a legal battle.

It is simply not true. This chapter will try to place contract law in a different perspective, because many small businesses cannot afford the legal protection a lawyer might consider minimal.

As a small businessman I ran an electronic component manufacturing company that had over 300 customers. Each customer insisted upon acceptance of his purchase order terms and conditions, and because the industry was very competitive there was no choice but to comply. At one time I read through about 100 different versions of these terms. They were appalling. My company had all of the responsibilities and none of the rights. Yet, in over four years, I never had a law suit and was able to resolve many nasty disputes in my company's favor.

To have negotiated special terms and conditions with each customer would have taken the full time of two attorneys at a cost approaching the company's total earnings. Several lawyers told me that the terms were all in the buyer's favor and were probably enforceable. So why did I not have any trouble?

Who you deal with is more important than what you sign

In the above case the customers were well-established, reputable companies in the aerospace and electronics industries. The wording in their purchase orders was severe because those companies did not want anyone taking advantage of them. Conversely, they had no desire to take advantage of anyone, particularly a small business. They would invariably give relief if it was reasonable. There were a few exceptions but these were known throughout the industry as tough customers and were handled differently. For example, prices quoted to the tough buyers were higher and delivery promises longer. Nor did we quote on items that were marginal from a profit standpoint.

Customer relations were based on a mutual regard for what was fair under the circumstances. At times we helped them out of delivery binds, and they remembered. If you have customers you know and trust it makes your business much simpler.

You deal with people, not corporations

The buyer, the purchasing agent, the contracts administrator, and even the division manager are all people. They want to do right by their company, but do not want to be ogres. You can deal with them on the basis of what is fair rather than what is legally obtainable. If you get a little more than the letter of the contract permits, it does not come out of their pockets. All they need is a way to explain it to the boss.

A word of caution

Because you deal with people, you must avoid any personal attack or any act that will degrade them in the eyes of their cohorts or superiors. Such a mistake will result in reprisals, legal and otherwise.

If you are dealing with another small businessman you must view him in light of your own needs. You cannot hurt him without his fighting back. Your legally superior position will not make him cave in to your wishes.

Contracts are not much good if the other party is bad

A common Mafia trick is to order large quantities of goods, sell them, and skip with the proceeds without paying any invoices. What good does a contract do?

Companies using private-line manufacturers have often been accused of capturing their suppliers. A good contract is no defense.

A company can go bankrupt owing you services or money.

Contracts are often unenforceable

It does a big company no good to cancel your order and hit you with reprocurement costs if it will drive you into bankruptcy. It wants only what you promised, not damages in lieu thereof.

Of course there are many cases when a contract will be enforced, such as when you try to back out of a special equipment order. These situations almost always involve intentional wrongdoing, however, and you should know what you are getting into.

Law suits take time and cost money

A major suit may take three or four years to come to trial. During the intervening years there will be interrogatories, depositions, and subpoenas. People in the company will have to gather facts and provide endless details about the dispute. The law firm will expect prompt payment of its bills. Even the big companies hate litigation and seek compromises.

Leverage

There is a lot of leverage that has little to do with the legalities. Suppose you believe you are entitled to added compensation for additional scope under the contract. The customer says you are wrong and directs you to continue to deliver under the contract terms. You can stop delivery and demand compensation, even though you know you are wrong. If the company needs the parts badly enough, it will give in. Of course, your prospects for future business are not good.

Contracts are rarely concise

Despite the attorneys, contracts usually have wide areas of ambiguities that never come to light unless there is a dispute. It does not take an attorney to find these weak spots. Once a weakness is found by the prospective defendant, the plaintiff is more apt to compromise.

Who has the cash?

The man with the money has the edge. If a buyer has paid for an item received, his position is weaker than if he has held up the invoice. If he rejects the item, it will take him four years to get his money back in a legal dispute. If he rejected the item prior to payment he will not have to pay for four years, even if he is wrong. By then he will have another job.

The man who wants the money is the one most willing to compromise.

Warning: *This tactic does not work with the U.S. government.*

Document!

The more paperwork you can produce to support your case, the stronger it will be. Try to get your position on paper before the event occurs. Be the first to write. It puts your adversary in a defensive position. If he does not answer, your case is strengthened. Your letters will also frighten his lawyers. No attorney likes to be out-documented.

If you are in a business where a buyer places orders by phone, send written confirmations. Although buyers rarely reneg on phone orders, there are often misunderstandings about exactly what was ordered. Put the buyer on the spot. Make him correct your reply, or it will stand.

Also when you are buying, be the first to confirm. Get that phone order in writing.

Trade practices

The way business is normally conducted in your industry has an important bearing on any dispute. Courts have frequently stated that a contract was modified by trade practice. The way you normally do business is the safe way.

The federal government

Federal statutes such as the Federal Acquisition Regulations make dealing with the government much different than dealing with private industry. The laws were written to minimize disputes between the government and the private sector. Certain aspects give the government an unfair bargaining position. For one thing, it can stop payment and demand restitution. You must comply.

The contracting officer is the official with the power to negotiate on the government's behalf. In addition he resolves disputes at the lowest level by making "findings of fact." Appeals from final decisions of contracting officers are made to various claims boards. Contractors filing claims have a high degree of success, but the procedure is definitive and must be followed specifically. Failing to make a proper objection in 30 days deprives the claimant of all rights, including the right to appeal.

Because the contracting officer has duties to both sides, he will tell you what you must do, if you ask.

If your company is engaged in government business it should have an employee experienced in contracting with the procuring agency to lead the way.

Big-company tactics

Large corporations are known to have a staff of house lawyers, so outsiders often believe that they can pursue litigation with very little cost. Sometimes companies trade on this belief for their own benefit. It is not true. For one thing, their law staff is not trained in litigation and has not been hired for that purpose. They usually hire outside firms.

Furthermore, top executives dislike getting tied up in lengthy depositions. They have better things to do.

When big companies litigate they like it to be on matters of their own choosing. Chances are you do not fit into that category, so do not let them scare you.

How to handle yourself

To avoid contractual problems you should:

- Know your customers. Stay clear of fast operators.
- Deal fairly with everyone.
- Do what you say you will.
- Maintain friendly relations with customer employees.
- Document everything.
- Get your money quickly.
- Do not be a pushover. Use leverage.
- Know when to call your lawyer.

When to call your lawyer

- When you are doing something that is not part of your day-to-day business, like signing a long-term loan agreement or buying a product line.
- When the potential risk is great and you are not sure of the other party.
- When you have a dispute that you are unable to resolve.
- When someone has wronged you (like refusing to pay a bill or arbitrarily rejecting your goods).
- When the other man has called his lawyer.

(Also see chapter 15.)

Do not neglect the contract

Even though a contract is prepared without the benefit of an attorney, that does not mean it should be handled sloppily. A contract should reflect the agreement of the parties, and if there is something in it that you do not like, *be certain* to have it changed *before* you sign. If you handle yourself carefully you will be able to live without lawyers except when someone is purposely trying to put one over on you. Lawyers are to protect you from people who do not deal in good faith. Most disputes arise between people who are honest but have misunderstood one another. In such a case you should be able to reach a satisfactory compromise even though you have no legal grounds for any remedy.

CONTRACT LAW

Now that you have learned all about contracts there are some things you should know about contract law.

What is a contract?

A contract is an agreement for *mutual* benefit. Both parties must receive something for their participation. This is called *consideration*. A *promise* is not a contract.

The uniform commercial code

The Uniform Commercial Code (UCC) is the body of law governing contract law. It has over a hundred sections governing sales alone. Most business law texts carry summaries of the code. You should buy one and read it. Or purchase the *Credit Manual of Commercial Law* from the National Association of Credit Management, 475 Park Avenue, New York, N.Y. 10016.

Parol evidence

To be sure you have a contract, write it down. In many cases oral agreements are not enforceable.

Document every agreement you make. A letter of understanding signed by you is written evidence of a contract.

Of course, follow through on your word as well. Many oral agreements are enforceable.

Misunderstandings

If the parties were not in agreement on the major portions of the contract, then there is no contract. It is *void*.

Minor disagreements

If the parties disagree on minor portions of the contract, then those parts are treated as if they did not exist but the contract is enforceable as to the parts that were agreed on.

This commonly arises on terms and conditions for a sale-purchase. The purchase order probably has words like these printed on the bottom of page one:

Terms and conditions printed on the reverse side (or attached hereto) are part of this purchase order. No variations can be made by seller's acknowledgment. Any changes hereto must be made by a purchase order revision. Seller acknowledges this provision by proceeding to perform.

The supplier returns a signed copy of the purchase order with a "subject to" written on it. He attaches his printed acknowledgment form:

Acceptance of this order is conditioned upon buyer's consent to terms and conditions attached hereto as sole terms and conditions of this order. Modifications shall be made only by mutual consent in writing.

The parties obviously have no agreement as to terms and conditions. If both sides ignore the conflict, as is likely, then the terms and conditions that do not agree are unenforceable but the major portion of the contract, that is, the goods to be delivered and the price, is very much in existence.

A standard paragraph similar to the one above is worth using when you accept an order. If you have a special product or if the contract you are placing is very large you may want to get the terms negotiated before you proceed, however.

Promises

Some promises must be kept. For example, if a party acts in reliance upon a promise and the promiser is aware of that, he cannot avoid obligation because of lack of consideration.

Modifications to contracts made by mutual consent are generally enforceable even though there was no consideration.

Silence

Silence is often consent. If a written confirmation is not rejected, objected to, or modified within ten days it becomes binding.

More than one contract between the same parties

You do not have the right to break a contract because the other party has breached another contract with you. For example, you cannot withhold delivery on a second order because the first has not been paid for.

Of course, most companies will do just that and will get away with it because that is an effective way of obtaining payment.

The UCC supplies the proper procedure for withholding shipment on the second contract, namely, making a written demand for *adequate assurance of performance.*

Remedies for breach of contract

The standard remedy for breach of contract is money damages. If damages are difficult to prove after the fact, they can be written into the contract ahead of time as *liquidated damages.*

The damages for failing to pay for goods delivered are simple enough: the price of the goods plus accrued interest.

For cancellation of a supply contract before delivery, the damages would be costs incurred plus anticipated profits. Costs would have to be verified by employee time cards or testimony, invoices paid, and overhead expenses prorata.

If goods ordered were not delivered or were not in accordance with the purchase order and were not rejected, the damages could be any monies paid for the goods plus additional expenses for placing the procurement elsewhere (reprocurement costs) plus secondary costs such as loss of time and efficiency. These secondary costs may be hard to prove but they are collectible.

Another remedy, allowed in special cases by a court of equity, is *specific performance.* One party may obtain a judgment requiring the other to give up a particular piece of land or a famous painting for which money would be no substitute.

Rejection of goods

A buyer has a right to inspect goods delivered and to reject them if found unsuitable. The buyer must state the nature of the rejection and must do so in a timely manner. He must state all objections simultaneously. He may accept partial shipments, separating the good from the bad.

Upon rejection the buyer should ship the units back to the seller, collect, unless the seller asks him to dispose of the goods for the seller's account. The seller is responsible for the shipping costs and for picking up the goods. Buyer must follow reasonable instructions of the seller to dispose of the goods, particularly if they are perishable.

Failure to make timely rejection

If the buyer does not reject in a timely manner, acceptance occurs. Rejection is a specific event. Telling the seller you are not happy with what you have received is not rejection. Stopping payment is not a rejection. You must tell the seller you do not want it and are sending it back. This must be done without undue delay. The time will vary depending upon how long a reasonable inspection should take and other circumstances.

Right to reject for late delivery

If you wish to reject for late delivery, the contract must be specific about that right and must clearly state what constitutes late delivery. A statement such as "time is of the essence" printed boldly across the purchase order also helps.

If you have been in the practice of accepting late deliveries or if you let much time pass before notifying the buyer that you no longer wish his goods, you may have waived your rights to reject for that cause. If you knew in advance about his delivery problems and urged him to continue performance, the same may be true. It is hard to make such a rejection stick when there are extenuating circumstances.

Right to reject for incomplete delivery

The buyer has a right to reject for incomplete delivery but he must give timely notice that the goods are rejected. He cannot use some, because this implies partial acceptance. He can give notice that the balance must be received before a specified date. The notice should state that the contract has been impaired by the inadequacy of the deliveries.

Minimizing damages

The aggrieved party has an obligation to minimize the damages of the party who has breached the contract. For example, if the purchaser informs you that he will not accept delivery of an uncompleted device, you cannot hurry up and finish it and then sue him for the original purchase price. You are entitled to costs up until the notification of cancellation plus anticipated profits. The costs spent completing the project are on you. What is more, you cannot force anybody to accept delivery.

Warranties

A warranty can be expressed or implied. Expressed warranties are written or otherwise agreed to between parties. There is always an implied warranty of suitability for the purpose intended, provided no buyer specification exists.

A supplier of a microwave oven implies that the oven will cook food. The food must be edible although it does not have to be the equal of food cooked in an ordinary oven. The microwave oven should not cause injuries or damage other objects.

If the buyer has a specification, the seller is responsible for meeting the specification but is relieved of the implied warranty for suitability.

In addition to suitability, the buyer receives an implied warranty for title, merchantability (if for resale),and possibly for safety. Such implied warranties may be denied by the contract between the two parties.

Warranties require the seller to fix, replace, or refund, usually at the seller's option. The buyer must give the seller such an opportunity.

Breaking a contract

A contract cannot be enforced and nonperformance is excusable when performance is impossible. Such impossibility must be clearly established. Extra costs or extra difficulty do not establish impossibility. A new statute that makes the performance of the contract illegal does constitute impossibility.

Contracts that are unconscionable can be unenforceable. Limitations on consequent damages for personal injury on sales to consumers is unconscionable. So is a *contract of adhesion*. This is a take-it-or-leave-it type deal where one side has all the bargaining power because of its size or market position. If one landlord owned all the apartments in town, his lease would probably be considered a contract of adhesion.

Contracts based on fraud are considered void, that is, never made.

Contracts may be void or voidable if there was an initial misunderstanding. If one party was aware of the misunderstanding of the other, the injured party can decide whether he wants the contract voided or enforced.

When both parties breach they will lose any rights in court.

RECAPPING THE CHAPTER

The day-to-day activity of most businesses involves buying and selling. The businessman should be able to survive this without legal help. That does not mean he should close his eyes to potential legal problems. Rather, he should try to head off problems and resolve them on a basis of what is the right thing to do. He should never be afraid to stick up for his rights. He can do a lot on his own if he tries.

17

LIVING IN A
COMPUTERIZED WORLD

A data explosion is under way as a result of the development of large-scale integrated circuits. Engulfed as we are by this expansion, we have no way of knowing how long it will last or how extensive it will be. It may end only when everyone carries the wisdom of the world on his wristwatch computer.

The early 1980s saw the rise of the personal computer for home and business use. Millions were bought each year for office applications. Upstart companies rose to prominence and then fell quickly into oblivion as IBM entered and took over the marketplace. Apple Computer, which started the trend, hung on to number-two position, but it is not clear that there will ever be a significant number three. Even Apple advertises itself as "the computer for the rest of us."

Concurrent with the growth of the computer, automated networked office systems such as those provided by Wang and Lanier, made typewriters obsolete and revolutionized filing for many companies.

The use of satellites permits data to be transmitted from computer to computer anyplace in the world in seconds. So, the expansion covers more than the ability to generate data; it covers the ability to transport it. The implications are just beginning to be felt.

Add to the real utility the fact that computers and terminals are now status symbols for administrators, secretaries, engineers, marketeers, buyers, accountants, and just about everyone not working on the factory floor or talking directly to the customer. You have to deal with all this. You must distinguish between the productive and the unproductive while undergoing a brainwashing by computer proponents.

What is a computer?

Generically, a computer is anything which manipulates data to perform a task. This definition covers adding machines, gasoline pumps, clocks, abaci, and hundreds of other simple devices. Now, when people say "computer," they are talking about an electronic general-purpose digital computer. This device, which first came into existence in the 1940s, is just a machine which adds, subtracts, stores, and fetches an enormous number of ones and zeros and does this at incredible speeds. Yes, all of the functions of today's monstrously effective mainframe computers which guide satellites, predict weather, forecast economies, and design fusion experiments do so with only those few operations. All of the higher mathematics is derived out of adding and subtracting ones and zeros. All computer instructions are coded by ones and zeros. The magic is that the electronics of the machine and its internal programs are set up in such a way that neither the computer programmer nor the user has to be aware of the existence of ones and zeros.

The section of the computer which makes all this possible is called the Central Processing Unit (CPU). Over the past ten years CPUs have shrunk dramatically in size and cost, while increasing in complexity and capability. This progress resulted from advances in the basic electronic element which does the computing, from vacuum tubes to transistors and finally to integrated circuits which combine thousands of circuit elements on minute wafer chips.

Memory devices, which store the information (in the form of ones and zeros) for use either in the computation process or as part of the user's data bank, have all shrunk in size and cost and grown in capacity. This also is due to the Large Scale

Integrated circuits (LSI) and Very Large Scale Integrated circuits (VLSI). Wafer-thin silicon chips approximately a quarter inch square now store over a quarter million bits of information. This is nowhere near what will be possible on that same size chip in the year 2000. The technology of the hardware has not stabilized. We are still experiencing geometric growth.

Bits and bytes

These terms are bandied about by all computer people, whether or not they know very much about computers. A *bit* is a binary signal, i.e., a one or a zero. It is almost always established by a voltage value, like over four volts being a one and under one volt being a zero.

A *byte* is a group of eight bits. One byte can be used to represent more than 2,000 numbers in our decimal system. Two bytes, tied together, can represent more than 4 million numbers and three bytes more than 6 billion. When you see that one little chip can hold more than 30,000 bytes, you can begin to get some idea of the power of modern machines. Bytes can be coded to give the machine instructions. Several instructions, like "get" or "store" or "read" or "print," can fit in one byte. The microprocessor, which is the smart chip of the CPU, is designed to work with groups of bytes. The first microprocessor was an eight-bit (one byte) device. Then came the sixteen-bit and today the thirty-two-bit (4 byte) processor. Tomorrow it is likely they will devise a new name for groups of bytes. This capability in the microprocessor establishes the amount of information which is processed in parallel (simultaneously) at the designated machine speed. The number of bytes is rising and the machine speed is increasing every year.

So, what do we have?

We have a hardware technology which is capable of pouring data out of any machine in quantities which can overwhelm its user. If you read on, you will see that the limitation of the computer is not how it is built but the people who tell them what to do.

Types of computers

Computers fall into fuzzy categories, based upon their memory size and the speed and computing power of their central processors. The largest computers are called *mainframes*. These are the big computers we still think of when the word comes up. They are used for the massive data banks of governments, industry, and universities. Uses are both scientific and general purpose. IBM has dominated this market since the early 1950s. There are other companies in this business, however, like Burroughs, Sperry, and Honeywell. Cray Research makes the fastest supercomputers for national laboratories and universities and special government scientific uses. In the next decade, we can expect competition from Japan and Korea.

Next to the mainframes are the *minicomputers,* or *minis,* which are also very powerful and capable of being networked to many remote terminals. After IBM, Digital Equipment Corporation is the largest of the minicomputer manufacturers, but it has many competitors, such as Data General and Hewlett Packard. Minis are often used as dedicated devices which control complex processes. They form part of many military systems and are used by other manufacturers as part of a larger system. In other words, they are not always sold to the end user. Minis are often part of the office automation system.

Personal computers are primarily stand-alone machines for the individual, although there is a growing tendency to network these as well. Personal computers can be tied to time-share services by modems and thus work as a smart terminal. The personal computer has limited memory and must get around this by using external memory devices like floppy discs and cassettes. Each floppy disc usually contains a program required for a single task. Information from the personal computer can also be stored on a floppy disc for recall when needed. Two read-write disc drives are common for personal computers, but additional drives can be added.

The smallest computer is called a *home computer,* and these have sold in large quantities for game playing. Increased memory and disc drives can make home computers the equal of a personal computer.

Terminals

A terminal is an input-output station for a computer. The normal operator-controlled terminal is composed of a CRT screen, a keyboard, and some electronics. There are other input gimmicks available, such as the *mouse,* light pens, touch screens, and joy sticks, which allow the user to make changes or enter information in a simple manner. Terminals are tied to computers in a variety of ways—direct wire, telephone wire using a modem, microwave links, and fiber-optic links. Mainframes may have thousands of terminals; minis, hundreds. Personal computers are integral terminal-computer devices but can also be used as a terminal to another computer.

A terminal can be no more than a telex printer, but it can also be a smart terminal, meaning it has computing capability of its own. Terminals can interface with instruments as well as with people. The on-board computer of a satellite is also the remote terminal of the ground control station, taking instructions and converting them into actions aboard the satellite.

Programs

A computer is an electronic idiot until it is programmed. Programming provides intelligence. There are many levels of programming from the most basic sub-machine language (programming with ones and zeros) to the assemblers and compilers, such as FORTRAN, COBAL, PASCAL, and BASIC (about fifteen in all) which are higher-level languages and are in fact programs to do programs. Each repetitive programming task is coded, and only the symbol is thereafter required to have the computer program itself. Without these higher-level languages most computers would be lying idle, waiting for their turn to be programmed bit by bit.

At present the computer industry sales dollar is about 80 percent software (programming) and 20 percent hardware. In 1965 the ratio was reversed. The performance and the quality of the hardware has been improving constantly. Not so the software. Many believe it is not much better now than it was years ago.

A General Accounting Office study conducted in the early 1980s stated that of all the software development contracts placed by the government, 50 percent were delivered but not used, 25 percent were paid for but not delivered, and 20 percent were delivered and used but only after extensive rework.

Attempts by the government to monitor and evaluate programs by requiring a structured hierarchical documentation system has had mixed results to date.

Programming, to the uninitiated, is unbelievably time-consuming and costly. It is easier to justify hospital costs related to major surgery than programming costs of a simple microprocessor controlled instrument.

Separation of programmer and user

Because programming is so time-consuming, the computer user can rarely do his own. If he is not knowledgeable about computers, he may expect more than the machine can deliver. If he hires a programmer, there will be a communications barrier which can be broken down only by extensive cross-discussions. The programmer must eventually come to think like the user. Large aerospace companies reverse this process by training systems engineers to program.

Most businessmen know something about programming but are not adept enough or do not have enough time to do their own. If the business is large, there will be in-house programmers. A small business usually relies upon canned programs which can be bought at a computer center. This is a way to avoid programmers.

Caution: *Doing your own programming can become addictive.* You can end up so intrigued with the computer that you forget your business!

Understanding programmers

The programmer is the intermediary between your problem and the machine problem-solving capability. He has been trained to program the machine efficiently and that is bad. People trained to do things efficiently rarely do things effectively. A programmer is trained to use as little memory as possible, to consolidate instructions and thereby reduce computing time and to provide key trouble-shooting elements within the program so that it can easily be debugged. Unfortunately, you need none of these. You need a program to solve your problem regardless of the memory used. Many programmers are incapable of understanding your problem much less solving it. You are at the mercy of the programmer because you cannot tell him what to do and you cannot monitor what he has done. You can only explain in broad terms what you want the computer to do.

Coming up with an effective program is an iterative process requiring extensive debugging even with the best of programmers. No program works well the first time. So, for the small businessman and for the worker or manager with a special task, the best solution is to adapt your methods to a program which has already been debugged. For the engineer with a special problem to solve, for which no published program is available, it is best to do his own programming even if he isn't that good at it. The time spent will be repaid when the computer does what he wants.

Why computers are often misused

The worst thing that ever happened to the computer is that business schools were among the first to become aware of their existence. On the premise that top management could do a better job for the company if it was provided with more information, the business schools devised Management Information Systems (MIS) courses and thereby substituted data for awareness. Since management indulges itself in nonsense of this type, MIS was quickly accepted by industry and MIS experts became sought after. As a result, a large portion of computer outputs provides top management with information they do not use except to show it to the investment community as a sign of their advanced management techniques. People who have much better things to do with their time are made to feed the computers so managers can see what they are doing. Once management sees it cannot digest all of the information in the forms of computer print-outs, it hires analyzers to simplify and condense the information. The analyzers, being no fools, ask for more inputs to entrench their position, thereby increasing the ratio of nonproductive work to useful work. Unfortunately, there is rarely any feedback to the workers who provided the inputs, telling them how they can do their job easier or better.

I have fretted over this for many years, but it was put into focus by the enlightening book, *In Search of Excellence.** The book stressed that successful companies have a minimum of reports and those they do have are taken very seriously. Management is primarily a matter of communicating directly with people doing work (management by walking around). So I offer this advice. Do not use computers for the convenience of managers, unless they have explicit assignments. An exception might be the airline tariff manager who must see what the competition is doing before setting rates and must do this on a daily basis. Use computers to make the workers' jobs easier. It is the material control clerk, the buyer, the design engineer, and the stockroom clerk who can benefit from a computer.

Computer coverup

Once a computer is instructed what to do, you will see only what it does. If the instructions were based on faulty logic, you will not know.

Here is an example of how a commonly used computerized production control system absolutely ensures late delivery of the end product. This system sets up a parts-ordering release based on average lead times for purchased items. For example, if the last five orders for capacitors used in an electronic assembly averaged 120 days from purchase order to receipt, then the computer released the part for purchase 120 days before it was needed. This sounds logical, but let us look closer. If the average lead time is used, then there is a fifty-fifty chance that the part will arrive late. If there are twenty such items in an assembly, the odds are over a million to one that at least one will arrive late, and about even that ten will be late. This system was meant to balance efficient inventory

---

*Thomas J. Peters and Robert H. Waterman, Jr., *In Search of Excellence: Lessons from America's Best-Run Companies* (New York: Harper and Row, 1982).

costs and reasonable delivery, but it fails on both counts. Inventory cannot be reduced if you do not deliver.

Other questionable computer uses

Every professional football team uses computers to tell its coaches how the opponent will react in any given situation. This can become incestuous. The opponent can predict, based on his own computer, what he is expected to do and can therefore do something else, like what he is least expected to do. I have to believe that it is the intuitive and imaginative coach who has the advantage and it is the motivated ball players who win. On the other hand, I would not dream of recommending that teams give up computers.

Computers are often used to evaluate people. There are benefits to this, but I am sure that neither Einstein nor Steinmetz would look good to a computer. When computers are used to evaluate human characteristics, they must be used carefully, skeptically, and with intuition. Particularly, they must be kept away from bureaucrats.

Sometimes computers are not practical but are used because they are there. A computerized material control system is almost always desirable in a build-to-stock manufacturing environment. It can be a disaster in a short turnaround job shop. What about the case where a company does both? Management usually forces the job-shop ordering to be done on the computer just like the rest of the business.

Computer success story

The computerized reservation systems of the airlines industry saved transportation from total chaos after government deregulation. With the Official Airlines Guide becoming obsolete a day after publication and over twenty CRT pages of fares from Los Angeles to New York alone, as just one example, how could a travel agent or reservations clerk keep track of fares, schedules, ticketing requirements, and space availability without a terminal?

In the United States more than 80 percent of the 28,000 travel agents and perhaps another 15,000 reservation clerks use computers. The majority use either the Apollo system of

United Airlines or the Sabre system of American. Regardless, every airline accesses every system with its own fares and schedules. The operator of an Apollo terminal can call up all fares and all schedules between any pair of U.S. cities and many pairs of foreign cities, as well as seat availability. Reservations can be made and tickets printed by use of a simple keyboard entry. Seat assignments can be made and boarding passes issued for some airlines. This is done almost instantaneously, like magic. The few travel agents who failed to sign up for such a system are rapidly becoming cruise specialists or tour guides.

Why is this such a success story? Because the systems were designed for use by the travel agents and reservation clerks, not the airline executives or the agency owners. Also there is direct feedback. When stuck, the agent calls a help desk. Too many of the same questions result in changes. Ask any travel agent what life would be like without the computer.

CAD, CADD, CAE, CAM

Computer Aided Drafting, Computer Aided Drafting and Design, Computer Aided Engineering, and Computer Aided Manufacturing are wonderful tools in the proper environment. Major detriments to their desirability are the initial high costs and the people resistance. It takes time to get them accepted and time to realize their benefits. For a long time it will seem that the overall costs are higher than before these devices were used.

Service bureaus

Service bureaus can take over your computer tasks without making you buy a computer. They will put terminals in your plant or work from simple hand-written event tickets. Most banks provide payroll services where all you have to input is the pay rates and hours worked. They deliver checks, tax accounting services and even a job cost breakdown, if needed. Many other services are available from a large number of companies, primarily of the accounting type. They rarely provide a customized solution to your problem. You must adjust to their programs. If such an adjustment is easy, then this may be the least costly, easiest solution to your problem.

Buying a personal computer

If you are engaged in repetitive bookkeeping, information retrieval, number crunching, following trends, or other routine tasks, a personal computer may be useful. Before you buy, remember that a large percentage of computers end up unusued or underused. The reason is that programs have fairly complex instructions which must be followed without deviation. The use of a comma instead of a semicolon results in a flashing "syntax error" on the screen. If you use the program on a regular basis, you will remember the rules. If you use it infrequently, it may drive you up a wall. So do not buy a computer to do many things on an occasional basis. Buy it for frequent use of a few programs.

Since the software is more important than the hardware, you should buy a machine which can use IBM or Apple Software, unless another machine has the program exactly suited to your needs. Spread-sheet-type programs like *Visicalc*™ and Lotus 1,2,3™ are most popular and have a broad range of uses. Most worthwhile are their "what-if" features, which allow you to change individual items and to see how this affects the whole chart. However, don't think that you can slip a disc into the machine and become an instant expert. It takes work. In the future, programs can be expected to be easier to use. If you have a fear of computers, you may want to wait until you find one which is comfortable.

Many mathematical programs are available for solving financial, accounting, and engineering problems. These are excellent if they fit your circumstances.

Data-base programs are available to help you retrieve information on customers, suppliers, stock, or almost anything you might put into a card file. However, unless you must retrieve it in different ways, the card file is probably better.

Every computer has a word-processor program, and you should certainly buy this. You will also need a printer to get hard copies. Dot-matrix printers are able to make legible copies and provide good graphics. More expensive daisywheel printers give typewriter-quality printing but are not good for graphics. Exotic laser printers can handle both.

Simple suggestions

- Do not replace any working system (manual or computerized) with an unproven system. Try the new system in parallel before discarding what you know works.

- The best time to upgrade is when you must add people. It may be possible to reduce your people needs.

- Do not generate reports which are not required, even though they cost little. Hidden costs of reports are high.

- Remember, many tasks are still done better without the computer.

A final word

Computers are wondrous devices. The world can no longer exist without them. Nevertheless, they have always been oversold. They will never give as much as the salesmen promises.

18

HEDGING YOUR BETS

INSURANCE

All companies carry insurance. State laws require that workers be protected by workman's compensation insurance. Social Security is old age insurance. Many states have compulsory disability insurance as well as unemployment insurance.

In addition to the compulsory types there are many other types of policies that must be considered. Of course you will not be able to carry everything that might seem advisable. The costs are too high. What you should do is list the priorities of the various coverages and match these against your funds. Insurance must be considered as a total package if you wish to make any sense out of it. A good business insurance broker will be of immense help in clarifying the picture for you.

Comprehensive liability

Top priority for any company is a general liability policy. It should be for enough to cover the size of the awards injured parties have been able to obtain, certainly no less than $500,000.

The comprehensive liability policy should cover:

- Personal liability for owners and employees (slander, libel, false arrest, etc.)
- Product liability (damages and injuries caused by an improperly designed or built product).
- Personal injury.
- Owned, nonowned, and rented automobiles and trucks.
- Medical payments.
- Unstated liability covered by an umbrella clause.

The founders and the owners should be named in the comprehensive liability policy. Also, your lease should be checked to see whether it has any specific requirements for lessee coverage.

Fire insurance

Fire insurance should cover building, fixtures, equipment, personal property, and *business interruption*. The amount of business interruption insurance should be enough to see you back in operation after complete building destruction.

Life and disability

Partnerships and small corporations should take out *key man* insurance on the owners. This policy, together with a partnership or stockholder agreement, will allow the survivors to purchase the shares of the deceased owners of the business from the heirs with the insurance proceeds. By establishing the exact price and providing the funds through the policy, the possibility of an extended disagreement is all but eliminated. The beneficiary of the key man policies is the company.

Most group insurance policies now offer a disability option, but the owners may want a supplemental policy to ensure full salary continuance.

Accident insurance

Blanket insurance coverage for employees traveling on behalf of the company can be obtained for a relatively modest charge. Such a policy usually has a double-indemnity clause for death that occurs as a result of a common carrier accident. Those who travel frequently are usually included by name, but all employees are covered, regardless of whether they are named.

Group insurance

With the cost of medical treatment rising constantly, it is impossible for the wage earner to set aside enough money to provide for serious family illnesses. As a result, group insurance has come to be expected as a condition of employment.

Most group policies cover hospital treatment, medical expenses, and associated laboratory costs. Major medical coverage for coverage above basic policy limits is now almost universal. Term life insurance, disability benefits, and dental coverage also are available.

Your broker should be checking rates from the major carriers so that you always have the best coverage for the premiums you are paying. Use only reliable insurance companies.

Bonds

You may need a bond for your employees (fidelity bond), for your customer (performance bond), for quotations (bid bond), or for your state and city sales taxes. Your insurance broker should be capable of getting these for you. The Small Business Administration may make it easier for your company to obtain a bond by guaranteeing up to 90 percent of the face value. Have your broker use this service.

Workman's compensation

Employees must be covered by a workman's compensation policy, but the owners of the business are often excluded unless specifically named. State laws protect the owners from employee claims in excess of the policy coverage.

Unemployment insurance

Unemployment insurance is provided by the state and is compulsory. Rates are usually determined by company experience. The more ex-employees on the unemployment insurance roles, the higher the company's premium. Therefore, fight all claims that are not legitimate. You will save money every payday.

Look for this: *In many states the company rate is determined by a book balance. It may be possible to lower your unemployment insurance rate by making a lump sum payment to the state. This may save in premium payments many times the amount of the lump sum payment in a single year. Check it out today.*

How much to pay?

Insurance sounds good when the salesmen explain it. Unfortunately, you will not be able to protect yourself from every contingency. Such employee coverage as workman's compensation, group insurance, and unemployment insurance is really a payroll-related expense. With social security these costs will average about 25 percent of the gross payroll. You should figure these as part of the labor costs. There is nothing you can do about them, anyway.

All other insurance should cost between 1 and 3 percent of annual sales. The smaller the company, the larger the percentage. Obviously, if your business is hazardous, the insurance costs will be higher.

Your broker

All brokers are nice fellows. You need one who is also knowledgeable and industrious. He must keep up with the latest types of coverage and be aware of carrier rates. There is a large difference between insurance companies in insurance costs for the same coverage. Your broker's job is to get you the top value.

19

THE GOVERNMENT —
FRIEND OR FOE?

The federal government has too much power, and there is little control over the abuse of that power. It is wielded in the name of justice and equality, making the crusaders even worse than the petty bureaucrats. One of the Great Lies—"I'm from the government and I'm here to help"—is no joke to a lot of businessmen. When dealing with the government, a businessman must move cautiously to avoid becoming an unnoticed casualty of some bureaucratic gyration. Here are some simple rules to follow:

Do not get anyone down on you

This is the first rule for dealing with the government: avoid making personal enemies.

It makes no difference what the grade level of the civil servant happens to be, no good can come from antagonizing him. I have seen vindictive inspectors bring a smooth-running manufacturing organization to a grinding halt. What is more, nothing could be done about it. Large companies may have the muscle to have obdurate government employees transferred or overruled. Small companies rarely do.

If the employee you have irritated happens to work for a regulating agency like the Occupational Safety and Health

Administration (OSHA), Federal Trade Commission (FTC), or SEC he may be able to originate a formal government complaint. Whether you have the financial resources to fight capricious complaints is not important to the government.

Do not make the government suspicious

This is a corollary to not making government employees angry. Not all actions are taken because of personal vendettas. Most are honestly derived. So keep the company skirts clean and cooperate with government officials. Make your company as inconspicuous as possible.

Never offer bribes

It is not that bribes never work, it is that they may backfire with disastrous results. If an official asks for some form of bribe, pretend you do not understand him or treat it as a joke. Do not report him unless you have powerful evidence, otherwise the offender will be protected and your motives and veracity attacked.

Small business power

In politics, power emanates from campaign funds and from votes. Small businesses contribute little of either, so they have little legislation on their behalf. The Small Business Act that created the Small Business Administration is a notable exception. Unfortunately, when the SBA battles other agencies, it usually comes out second best. Few congressmen help small businesses, although almost all have made impassioned speeches in front of an empty chamber in order to get their position on small business entered into the *Congressional Record*. Republican or Democrat, it makes no difference. Each projects itself as the friend of small business; the former because it is "business" and the latter because it is "small." When the time comes to vote, neither will be a supporter.

There is nothing indicating a change. Whatever laws are passed are going to be window dressing at best.

The Small Business Administration

By the time you read this, the SBA may have fallen to the economy spree. Its loss will not be keenly felt. Even though the SBA was a friend, it was an ineffectual one. The SBA provided guidance (sometimes good), financial support, and help in getting government business. It also guaranteed performance bonds on government contracts. What will happen to government-guaranteed small business loans, to small business set-asides, and to Certificates of Competency once the SBA is eliminated is anyone's guess. If the agency survives, you may find them helpful at times, but don't expect them to win any interagency battles for you.

Equal Access to Justice Act

This new law, effective in late 1982, makes it possible for small businesses to obtain some recovery of their legal fees if they can show they were unfairly treated by the federal government. To be eligible, the aggrieved party must overcome the government's position in court, in administrative proceedings, or by settlement.

Appeals by the government delay such payments and largely circumvent the law's intent. Also, the payment cannot be obtained if the government's case is a good one, even though it lost.

The biggest benefiters will probably be the attorneys, although it is too early to say.

Procurement agencies

Federal law requires that small businesses be given high priority in government awards, but this is largely circumvented by most procurement groups. Buyers do not like to have their freedom of choice restricted and then to be held responsible for the results of going to a small company, particularly after they have been burned a time or two. They will try to get around the Small Business Officer, will fight small business set-asides, and will be obstructionists while giving all outward appearances of cooperation. They are pretty good at it.

One large supply depot that is extremely antagonistic to small business suppliers nevertheless gets more than its share of awards for small business participation. Every year it splits up the contracts held for small business into smaller pieces and then reports on the percentage increase of awards.

Of course, private industry is similarly reluctant to do business with its smaller brethren. The way to overcome this with both groups is by doing good work and building long-lasting relationships.

General Accounting Office

The GAO is an agency responsible directly to Congress, chartered to be a watchdog over government procurement practices. If there is any reason to suspect that your company has been unfairly treated in an award proceeding, you can appeal to the GAO. On large awards, appeals have become routine. They are rarely advisable for small contracts unless the offense has been blatant. Awards are rarely overturned and the appeal is likely to make a few enemies.

Types of government contracts

The government can purchase goods and services on a cost reimbursement basis or by a fixed-price contract. To be awarded a cost type contract you must have an approved accounting system and a satisfactory method for accumulating costs. If the contract is fixed-price but awarded without competitive bidding, you must be prepared to justify your estimates of costs.

The government must provide small companies with progress payments if requested. This will pay up to 90 percent of incurred costs even on fixed-price supply contracts. It is a form of financing and should be utilized. To qualify you must have an approved accounting system. Your costs will be audited.

If the contract is awarded by competitive bidding and you do not ask for progress payments, you do not need cost records. However, if the contract is terminated you must be able to prove your costs in order to establish a claim.

Types of competitions

Government awards may come as a result of a Request for Proposal (RFP), an Invitation to Bid (ITB), or a combination of the two, called a *two-step*.

An ITB is a straight price competition between approved suppliers. It must be advertised in the *Commerce Business Daily*. Bids are sealed and opened immediately after bid closing. The lowest price wins the contract.

An RFP is a competition based on other factors as well as price. The request will explain the factors to be considered and their relative weights. The contracting officer may narrow down the choices as he determines what best suits the government's interests and negotiates price and performance with the remaining competitors, finally picking a winner.

The two-step is a procedure requiring competitors first to qualify technically. After entrants are qualified the second step is a straight price competition.

The laws are established to provide the maximum advantages of competition to the government and they have been effective.

Regulating agencies

Government agencies have been established over the years to prevent businesses from engaging in activities that are against the public interest. There is nothing wrong with the concept, but the laws often discriminate against businesses that cannot afford the legal costs to battle arbitrary directives. It costs more than most small companies can afford just to keep up with government directives (often called "agency law.") Installing an approved accounting system may itself be an onerous burden. Large companies take these directives in stride, passing the increased costs on to the customer.

Some of the more powerful agencies are the:

- Securities Exchange Commission—responsible for control of the sale of securities.

- Federal Trade Commission—responsible for fair competitive practices.

- Occupational Safety and Health Administration—responsible for safety standards and enforcement.

- Equal Opportunities Commission—responsible for fair employment practices.

- Department of Labor—which monitors wage and hour laws.

- National Labor Relations Board—which monitors union-management elections.

- Internal Revenue Service and the U.S. Customs Service—which are collection agencies.

- Defense Contract Compliance Agency—which monitors the compliance of defense contractors with federal laws.

What to do when under investigation

If you have been accused wrongly by a government agency, it is not necessary to run to an attorney. Try getting a little help on your own, first. Check with the investigating officer. Get the names of his superiors. Visit them and present your side of the case. Stop at the local Small Business Administration Office. Ask for their help. Visit your congressmen and senators. See whether their staffs will help. If you can present your case clearly and without excess emotion, you will be surprised how much help you can muster.

Put pressure on the investigator to drop the case. Make him worry about his own career without making any direct threats. Take voluminous notes of any conversations and then confirm these in writing, sending him a copy. Act angry and indignant.

Whatever happens, do not lie to anyone. A single fib can destroy your position and make it impossible for your friends to help you. Remember, they will want to end up as good guys for protecting the innocent, not as unwitting cover-up collaborators.

Obviously, you do not conduct life-and-death matters without professional help. Use a little judgment.

Congressmen

Your congressman may not vote for small-business legislation, but when the chips are down he will be your biggest supporter and your most effective ally in the battle with government bureaucracy. The help that a Representative provides his constituents in dealing with red tape is a source of great personal satisfaction to him. After all, he does not sponsor many new bills. Moreover, the help is apolitical. It does not matter which party you support.

A congressman can get through to top agency officials where you cannot. He can demand an explanation. He can draw attention to iniquities. Most agencies must log all congressional inquiries and respond within a given time. The item will be investigated. Of course, department goofs are likely to be covered up, but the final result may redress a wrong.

Although most agencies are thrown into a tizzy by a congressional inquiry, a few, particularly the Department of Defense, resent them and go into a routine that is calculated to frustrate the complaining party without giving him legal grounds to complain further. In other words, he gets "the treatment." Such agencies are too good at this sort of thing to be smoked out. Congressional influence may be unproductive, but it does no harm to exercise a little political influence (PI) if you have already exhausted the official channels of complaint.

Tax audits

Thousands of business audits are made yearly. The IRS investigator expects to find some discrepencies. He cannot waste too much time drilling a dry hole, however. His opinions are his own and are subject to challenge, so long has you have concealed nothing on the return. If you make him understand you intend to appeal, he will be inclined to negotiate a settlement.

Your accountant who made out the return should defend it against any IRS challenge. He should be there with you. Tell him you expect him to fight, not acquiesce. If there is any backtracking to be done, you should be the one to do it.

Appeal

There is a procedure for appealing almost all government directives or findings. Usually the official sending the notice will supply information regarding appeals. Watch out, though. Most appeals have a thirty-day time limit. After that you have no further rights and must comply. If you do not like the directive but do not know what to do about it, do not dally; send a letter back to the originator even if you are not certain what you want. Say that you object to the findings and appeal the decision to higher authorities for a reversal. Be positive; use the words "object" and "appeal." This should get you safely into the appeal channel. Keep a copy of the letter; have it witnessed. Send the original by certified mail and retain the receipt.

If the matter is very important get an attorney. If it is not so important and the expense of legal help appears prohibitive, consider appealing on your own. Most appeal proceedings can be followed and conducted by laymen, and the law allows for it. In many cases there is everything to gain and little to lose by appealing.

Document

Dealing with the government is much easier if everything that transpires can be proved by documentation. The documents need not be formal. Letters to the contracting officer, internal memos, memos for the file, time cards, purchase orders, cancelled checks, and expense records all are forms of documentation. If you decide to appeal, get written statements from all parties. Do not rely upon oral testimony. The appeals board or hearing officer will probably not keep a transcript of the hearings but all documents submitted in evidence become a part of the case record. Consequently the decision indicated by the preponderance of written evidence is most likely.

Unfair competition

The Federal Trade Commission is responsible for monitoring competition and providing remedies for unfair practices. Under FTC jurisdiction are such acts as price fixing, tie-in sales, false advertising or promotion, palming-off (passing off goods as those of a competitor), false labeling, etc.

Other types of unfair competition are more in the nature of civil torts than violations of a public trust. These are the theft of trade secrets, violations of trademarks, and disparagement of another's product. Redress can be obtained in a court for these acts, whereas the FTC has the authority to issue "cease and desist" orders as well as to require corrective advertising.

Severe penalties can be imposed on those convicted of price fixing, even on a local basis. Keep records of major pricing decisions. Also, be sure that you charge every customer the same price for a similar quantity of the same product. Any discriminatory form of kick-back is illegal.

The future

The future is not encouraging. Although the Reagan administration has made strides in deregulating certain industries with mixed results to the consumer, an ominous trend is developing related to government procurements. This movement is largely the responsibility of Congress, but there are many bureaucrats supporting it. I am talking about the legislation which has been proposed to limit profit on individual contracts, the stripping away of proprietary rights, and the requirement for unreasonable warranties. Some of the proposed laws would make the losing contractors responsible for government legal costs while not giving the contractor the identical right to obtain legal costs from the government. These items will be disproportionately harmful to the small businessman and might eventually make business with the government undesirable.

In any event, business owners must learn to cope with the increased bureaucracy by getting to understand the laws. Otherwise, he will be caught between the possibility of citations on one hand and overpowering legal costs on the other.

20

CRISIS MANAGEMENT

Businesses fail. Everyone who has his own business is aware of that. Whether yours is one of the fortunate ones depends on two things: luck and you. Nor are the two variables independent. As any gambler (and a businessman is a gambler) can tell you, it does not pay to fight luck, you must bend with it.

The growth of supermarkets during the late 1940s put most of the independent grocers out of business. That is luck. And yet many of the independent grocers saw the start of this trend and began their own chains of supermarkets. These men had foresight, ability, and enough luck to obtain financing when they needed it.

Today, in thousands of neighborhood shopping malls throughout the country, independent shops compete successfully with adjacent department stores. Others struggle and die in neglected, rundown city centers, which once provided a plethora of customers. In still other cities, motivated merchants helped restore their neighborhoods and brought customers back.

So, the success of your business will depend upon you. There is no other course than to do the things that improve the odds on surviving.

Causes of failures

Most failures are caused by the inability or the unwillingness of management to appraise the circumstances objectively and to take corrective measures. This happens more frequently because of emotional weaknesses than from a lack of native ability. People hate facing up to decisions that may result in an uprooting of the company that has absorbed so much of their life's effort.

Immediate causes of business failures are lack of sales, insufficient margin, and inadequate capital. The situation may be temporary or permanent. Adept managers can sense changes and take steps to meet the new challenge. This is what owning your own business is all about.

Falling sales

Buying habits are always in a process of change. Some of these changes result from unexpected events. The switch to smaller automobiles was brought about by the 1973 war in the Middle East and the oil embargo. Although the war was short, the change is a long-term one.

The movement of the affluent from cities to suburbs brought the rise of the elaborate shopping mall. Both the cause and the effect were gradual but continuous. Great sociological improvements must come about before this trend will be reversed.

Products come and go with technological innovations. Swiss movements are being upstaged by integrated circuits. Slide-rules have been made obsolete by hand-held calculators. Your product may be next. Are you ready?

A new store may open up down the street and take away half your business in the first month. This is a localized event, having no general market implications. It requires a unique solution.

You may have brought about your problems on your own. Poor quality or discourteous employees may have driven away your customers. Your solution lies within.

Analyze the situation

Before you can make a decision you must collect and assimilate facts. If you have been on top of your marketing tasks, these facts are already on hand.

Is the business drop-off universal? Figures from the Department of Commerce and your trade publications will provide some guidance. Check with trade organizations, salesmen, customers. Attend trade shows and mix with the competition. Get out and count the cars in your competitor's parking lot.

If the answer is yes, seek the cause. The cause will tell you whether the change is likely to be permanent. Are customers doing without? If so, the drop in business is likely to be temporary. Have they found another solution to their needs? This would be cause for serious concern. Is the solution better than the one you offer, or will customers try it and then come back to you? Have their priorities changed? Has the economy caused them to eliminate luxuries?

Your customers should tell you, if you listen carefully, whether your problem is self-induced. Even though they don't tell you so, you may assume that it is if the general business trend is still healthy while you are suffering. Is your product at fault? Your prices too high? Your service poor? Are your customers treated the way you would like to be treated? Any outside consultant will answer these questions for you in a couple of days if you feel you are too close to the problem.

Of course, it may be that the competitor down the block is giving you fits. If so, why is he getting business that could be coming to you? Does he have lower prices? Better surroundings? Superior service?

Do not close your eyes to the painful truth. There is no escape from the reality of the situation. Your only hope is to focus on your deficiencies and eliminate them.

Long-range changes

Long-range changes demand long-range, fundamental responses. You may have to move your business or change your product line. Perhaps you can turn the tide with a change in your manufacturing or merchandising methods. Fortunately, most basic changes come about slowly, so if you recognize the trend far enough in advance you can plan your response.

Making a basic change requires the self-assurance that comes from a thorough knowledge of your business and confidence in your own ability to adapt. Delay can be fatal. Small companies do not have unlimited resources. If you wait until your reserves dwindle, it may be too late to make that move or develop the new product.

Temporary changes

If business is on a temporary or cyclical downturn, tighten your belt and wait it out. When a gambler is losing, he shortens up on his bets. He does not double up. The time for building the pot is when the lucky streak is going.

Recessions are the opportunity to get rid of the deadwood, improve the efficiencies, and eliminate the frills. This can be a healthy period for your company in the long run. Whatever happens do not throw your reserves against the general trend. You will have nothing left to take advantage of the good times ahead.

Local competition

Do not react in panic when the new competitor takes away a chunk of your business. You must fight on your terms, rather than on his. Once again, explore the possibilities. Your competitor is starting out, replacing an existing business, or expanding. He may be acting wisely or foolishly. His business may or may not be adequately financed. His lower prices may be based on lower costs, in expectation of higher volume, or on ignorance. It is up to you to determine which.

Even if he has had a record of success and is adequately backed, he cannot take all your business away unless you let him. You, too, can lower prices and gird for a long fight. If you can hold out you may discover that the market can support you both.

Concentrate on selling your strengths. Give the best service you know how. If possible, specialize. Get better at a few things. If you have a clothing store, concentrate on a variety of blouses, perhaps. Carry quality products and promote them vigorously. Chances are that your competitor will give you this edge without a fight. You are in a way dividing the market, but at the same time trying to enlarge it. This is the way that most competitors come to co-exist.

Driving business away

Many business owners are their own worst enemies. They allow their businesses to be conducted for their own benefit or for the benefit of the employees rather than for the customers' satisfaction. If business is good all around you and if you have a salable product, you are obviously doing something wrong. Get help. You need it. You have let things slide without knowing it and you must get the blunt facts from someone you can trust. This is what consultants are for, if you will listen to them. The fact that you pay for their advice may make it easier to swallow. It won't be easy, though. No one likes to be told he has goofed, an entrepreneur least of all. But you should assume the worst until shown otherwise.

When profits are down

If your sales are holding steady, even building, but the cash is dwindling, you can look inward for the solution. You are pricing too low or spending too high. You must fix one or the other. For a quick fix, try raising your prices just a little. Meanwhile collect facts. Find out what people are paying for your competitors' products. If you are running a bid-and-award type business, check your capture rate. There is such a thing as winning too many. Let your competitors share in the underpriced end of the business.

Take a look at your costs. Are you paying too much for what you are buying? Can you group your purchases and get a lower price? Have you checked all the sources? How about your manufacturing processes? Are they up to date, or are you clinging to old methods? While the world around you has been changing, have you been standing still? Do not shrug it off. It takes a masochistic self-analysis to keep from falling by the wayside.

When you are short of funds

When you need money the worst, you will find the least. So get your house in order before going to the bank for a loan. If you show them what you have done for yourself, they will be most likely to respond. Here is what you can do:

- Stretch payables. Tell your suppliers you are in a temporary bind. Promise them payment by a specific date, then hold to the promise. If you have one or two large creditors, see whether they will take promissory notes.

- Get busy accelerating collections. Ask for fast payment. Tell your customers you must have it. Give discounts, if necessary, but do not take no for an answer.

- Cut back on inventory. Sell off excess at a discount or even to a surplus dealer.

- Reduce expenses. Put off every purchase possible. Cut back on the payroll or on the work week if business permits. Otherwise eliminate all unnecessary overhead. Do not cut back on selling costs unless you can do so without affecting sales. Many companies make advertising the first casualty, a drastic error.

- Sell off excess capital equipment or a marginal product line.

Make a detailed list of the actions you have taken and the costs you have eliminated. Take it to the bank with your loan request.

Your biggest problem

Let's face it. If you did not have an inflated ego, you would still be working for someone else. It is a mixed blessing, however. A few years of success will provide an executive with more than some dollars in the bank. It may give him an unshakable sense of infallability. When the chips are down, this trait may prove his downfall.

Executives have been known to ignore all the distress signals, simply because they cannot comprehend that they may have acted incorrectly. They will go on doing the same thing at a renewed pace on the premise that if one won't do it, two will. They will find some reason to rationalize why the fundamentals simply do not apply in their case. The observer, they believe, will be incapable of understanding the problem.

This kind of compulsive reaction has resulted in the failure of many companies that otherwise could have been saved. It affects executives of large companies as well as small ones. In fact, it is the reason why few chief executives have successfully pulled off turnarounds in their companies and why most must be replaced after a bad year or two.

If you own your business there is no rescue team waiting in the wings. As Truman said, the buck stops here. You have to be equal to the task. If your business is in trouble it is because you did something wrong, in all likelihood. Facing up to that is not an easy assignment.

21
GROWING BIG

The majority of businessmen would like nothing better than to be able to make their company very large. Although aspirations vary, every entrepreneur will tingle at the thought of running a billion-dollar corporation. The funny part about this is that such success is more apt to be random luck than great vision. Unfortunately, the founder is likely to be replaced along the way by a professional manager selected by his financial partners. Despite this, his personality may make a permanent imprint upon the company.

Why founders are replaced.

The most common reason is that the attributes of a promoter-entrepreneur are not those of the large company executive. It is primarily the difference between doing things yourself and doing them with a large unwieldy organization.

There are other reasons, of course. One is a breakdown of the relationship between the financial backers and the founders. If these two groups are on unfriendly terms, the company managers are not likely to survive a downturn.

The inexperience factor is important. Entrepreneurs are not likely to admit that they do not know how to run their own company, but they may have had zero management experience elsewhere.

Danger points along the way

The first challenge comes when the founder can no longer stay in touch with all the details. He can continue to demand that he review all of the activities and thereby slow the operation to a crawl. The necessary alternative is to delegate responsibiilty for various functions.

The next make or break point comes when he finds that large segments of his business are completely out of his control, even though he is the boss. The company seems to be running in spite of him. This is his opportunity to build up his personal staff and to exercise his control through them. Choosing such a route almost ensures disaster, since the people who do the work are deprived of necessary authority to get it done.

Finally, in all probability, he will come to the situation where he is in over his head and is not capable of participating at such grandiose levels because he has never been trained to do so.

Obviously, there are some founders who survive throughout the entire process simply because they are good and they keep their head about them. They develop a management style and a personal poise which weathers well.

How to survive

To see it through from beginning to end, from small to large, in good times and bad, here are some suggestions;

- Spend most of your time appraising the work of others.

- Get the best people.

- Remember that not all of your faithful employees can grow into the next level. It is all right to have a promote-from-within policy once you are large, but it won't work during rapid growth.

- Keep your credit lined up to cover your anticipated cash flow. Do not cut yourself adrift from your money.

- Cultivate your sources of capital. Do not antagonize your backers.

- Never promise more than you can deliver.

The entrepreneur and the financier

This is the scenario for the classic confrontation. If the company does well at the start, the founder resents the gains the financier is making simply for putting up a few bucks. He would like to squeeze him out at a discount. If the company does poorly and needs more money, the owner resents having to give more equity.

The other side of the coin is that employees of the financial institution often envy the entrepreneur's success, and some angle to be his replacement should the circumstances warrant. The financial group takes a hard line when a soft hand might be better. While they are in a venture for mutual benefit, the potential for conflict is great. The money-man usually wins.

If the entrepreneur treats the backers as benefactors and partners, he will serve his own case better. Common trust and goodwill is essential.

Develop style

In a small company, substance is everything. As the company grows, the manager finds what he says means less and less and the impressions he makes more and more. Good people rarely like to be told how to do things, but they are quick to emulate traits they think admirable. That is why the top man must have a management style and a set of values for others to follow. I have known executives who had their desks and chair on a slightly raised platform to give them an appearance of superiority, but this is not the style I recommend. You can recognize executives with style immediately. Dave Packard has it. Lee Iacocca certainly has it. Harold Geneen had it. Anyway, all I am saying here is that successful chief executives are good actors.

Make your imprint

Even though you do not survive in body, you can survive in spirit. You do this by setting the tone and the character of the business. These will survive not only you but also your successors, and it may help your company through trying times.

Summarizing: If you want to last in a growth environment you must let go some of the reins. You have to have good people around you. You must have money behind you.

22

GOING PUBLIC
FOR THE FIRST TIME

Everything changes, once a company is publicly owned. Expenses skyrocket, management spends more time placating the government, the stock brokers, and the stockholders than it does running the business. And worst of all, these same groups second-guess everything. As time goes on, things get worse.

Is it worth it? Not like it used to be. Every day more companies think about going *private,* but that is much harder than it sounds.

During the 1960s many little companies went public, some before they had even opened their doors. Not so, today. Now a company should be at a $10-million annual sales level before it thinks about this new burden.

Why go public?

In spite of the disadvantages, companies continue to have stock offerings. There must be some advantages.

- A public offering is still the best way to sell common stock, which increases capitalization without increasing debt. You get money that costs no interest and does not have to be repaid.

- Public stock has long been a form of currency for acquiring other companies.

- Founders can cash in on some or all of their holdings. Even if they do not sell, the public market places a value on their holdings, which can then be used as collateral.

- Founders can sell a portion of the company to others without losing operating control or any of the other personal benefits they enjoy.

- The new equity capital can be leveraged to increase the borrowing power of the company.

Disadvantages

- Too much management time is diverted to non-profit-making activities.

- Expenses increase, particularly nonproductive expenses.

- Government control increases.

- It is harder to keep secrets because of SEC disclosure rules.

- The company is subjected to harassment by dissident shareholders, special-interest groups, and even government agencies.

- Directors and officers have higher risks for personal liability.

- The equity of the founding group is diluted.

- The price of the stock becomes more important than the way the business is run.

What to do?

Be the reluctant groom. Put it off as long as possible. The larger the company, the easier it will be to absorb the new chores.

Ways to go public

- An S-1 registration. This is a full-blown offering, one that meets all the requirements of the 1933 and 1934 Acts. It is the best, although the most costly, way to go public. There is no limit on the amount of money that can be raised or on the number or location of stockholders (subject to state *blue-sky* laws). It is the only practical way to raise more than $500,000.

- An *intrastate* offering. Because the SEC's jurisdiction is limited to interstate commerce, it can be circumvented by selling stock within a single state. Courts have ruled that the stock must come to rest within the state in which it was sold. Brokers cannot solicit out-of-state buyers in the after-market. This may be an inexpensive way of raising a small amount of money, and it used to be popular for small companies. Reputable underwriters no longer wish to be associated with intrastate issues. It is considered a schlock operation. If there is another way to raise funds, intrastate offerings should be avoided because they hurt the chances of follow-on issues.

- A Regulation "A" offering. This is an exempt transaction under the 1933 Act. It is a small-scale S-1, with a registration statement and a prospectus but without many of the other details of an S-1 filing. The maximum sum that can be raised is $500,000 (before expenses are deducted). A Regulation "A" is often preferable to an intrastate offering but, like it, may hurt future financing. Companies that have had Regulation "A" issues may find it impossible to get brokers to make a market in their stock during times of low public interest in buying securities. As a result the price tumbles regardless of how the company is actually performing.

- Back-door distribution. A company can go public by acquiring a public corporation in a stock-for-stock transaction. This method still has a bad name from its abuse by high-flying conglomerates in the early 1970s. It has the further disadvantage of getting the acquiring company involved with hopeful stockholders without any means of fulfilling their expectations. The back-door stock distribution should be the byproduct of a desirable merger, not a means of going public.

Which way to go?

Get the best underwriter, the best SEC attorney, and a national CPA firm and come out with an S-1. In the long run you will be way ahead. If you cannot make an S-1, stick with private placements.

Getting ready

The time to get ready for an S-1 is the day you incorporate. Here is what to do.

- Get the financial statements audited by a CPA. Three full years are required (or from inception if that is less). Having a national firm at the start will make life easier.

- Maintain complete records of all major transactions (leases, large contracts, capital equipment purchases, etc.) and all matters related to the company's stock.

- Avoid special classes of stock. Stick to common.

- Keep complete records of sales, earnings, new orders, and backlog by product line and by customer so that prior years' results can be reconstructed.

- Keep accurate minutes of all director and stockholder meetings.

- Attach to the minutes copies of all contracts approved by the board.

- Keep copies of all forecasts. If they were distributed outside the company, have a record of to whom, when, and why.

- Have the sales department make a yearly analysis of the market for the company's products and the major competitors. Keep estimates of the company's market share, bid capture rates, and other significant marketing information.

- Keep up-to-date résumés of key personnel, showing all significant achievements.

- Maintain copies of all stockholder communications.

- Keep information relating to product reliability and customer acceptance, such as letters of endorsement, inspection reports, government and customer plant survey reports.
- Maintain a file of newspaper and magazine articles about items related to the company business, particularly if the articles quantify the total market.

All this sounds like a lot of unnecessary work. It won't be, if the company goes public. The reduced legal fees will more than pay for the effort.

Note this: *Probably half of the SEC attorney's efforts will be spent looking for material he suspects you are concealing from him. Every omission or inconsistency must be explained before he will be willing to represent you to the SEC. You can save a large portion of this effort if you come in prepared.*

GOING PUBLIC

This chapter is not going to guide you through a step-by-step procedure for going public because that is the job of your attorney and your underwriter. If you wish details, ask your financial printer for a copy of his handbook on securities law. You will find it an excellent source of information. I am going to cover the things that the chief executive must do to get good results and to keep costs down.

Getting started

Before you seek out an underwriter you must have an extensive five-year business plan and the best SEC attorney in town. Do not penny-pinch or short cut on either one, because you will want to attract the very best investment banker to manage your underwriting and you will want to make the best possible deal with him. That can happen only if he gets excited about your company and if you have someone on your team to negotiate an agreement for you.

Take note: *The success of the offering and the subsequent after-market depends as much on the managing underwriter as it does on the company performance.*

How to sell an underwriter

Do not shop around. With the help of your attorney and your banker, list the investment bankers that might be willing to handle your account in order of preference and go after them one at a time. Here is what you must tell each one:

- Your company has an excellent track record.

- The future promises to be even better. His clients will profit through their association with your company.

- Management is experienced and responsible. It will honor its obligations to the public stockholders.

- The company will be candid and aboveboard with the underwriter at all times, even when the news is unpleasant.

The first meeting with the underwriter is the most important. You must get your message across in as few words as possible. It is "Don't miss this opportunity." The five-year plan you leave with him must substantiate the message in detail. Remember, it is the back-up data and source material that makes it credible. It is easy to blue-sky numbers.

If your plan has been created by your employees, when the underwriter visits your plant his initial impression will be confirmed. What he sees and hears will dovetail with the words he has read. If the plan is the figment of some person's fertile imagination, it is likely to be undermined by your own people.

The work begins

Once the underwriter has agreed to take you out, the work begins in earnest. A registration statement must be drawn up, a prospectus prepared, a blue-sky survey made, the year-end audit and necessary stubs completed, a transfer agent and registrar appointed, and questionnaires filled in by officers, directors, and 10 percent of the shareholders. Documents must be accumulated and sent to the SEC attorney's office for review.

The chief executive should appoint executives to spearhead certain efforts. The treasurer should be responsible for all financial information and for directing the auditors. The secretary may be assigned to collect all documents. One of the vice-presidents may be assigned the task of writing the first draft of the prospectus, except for the financial sections. Another can follow progress and report when items lag.

The all-hands meeting

Early in the program the underwriter will request a meeting of the company's officers, the company's attorney, the CPA, any selling stockholders, the underwriter, and his counsel. The company's attorney should take the lead at this meeting and set forth the various tasks and their timetable. One of the company's officers should follow up and see that the job gets done, just as if he were an expediter.

Finding a printer

There is no way to have a public offering without the services of a first-class financial printer. There will be changes on the registration statement and on the prospectus right up until the last minute. There is an SEC "deficiency letter" that must be satisfied, in addition to the pricing amendment that must establish the exact price of the stock and the underwriter's commission. The printer must work all night before the effective date of registration to make these changes. No ordinary printer could handle the job. The cost of printing is extremely high, rivaling the legal and accounting fees. In fact, your lawyer and accountant will probably volunteer that the printer is the only one making money on the offering.

Your attorney will recommend printers with whom he has worked. Your underwriter also may have some recommendations. If you have a choice, pick one who offers a good securities regulation handbook. It is a valuable tool and is provided without cost.

A word about the registration statement

Every signer of the registration statement and every director, whether or not he signs it, is responsible for the accuracy of the document. The standards applied to due diligence exceed those normally applied to officers and directors. The president, because of his position and his authority, cannot expect to avoid personal liability for any material misstatement. All directors, especially the inside directors, will have similar exposure.

Make certain the registration statement is accurate.

AFTER YOU ARE PUBLIC

If, after the public offering, your company has total assets over $1 million and more than 500 shareholders, it comes under the reporting requirements of section 12 of the 1934 Act. It must now submit to the SEC quarterly reports (Form 10Q), annual reports (Form 10K), and material changes on a current basis (Form 8K). These must be made available to stockholders on request. The company must send annual and interim reports to stockholders and must follow the 1934 Act in preparing and submitting proxies and proxy statements.

Any event significant enough to affect the stock price must be made public on a timely basis by release to the newspapers and wire services. The company cannot conceal material facts without risking SEC action.

Reporting requirements seriously affect the ability of a company to keep trade secrets. Such things as sales and earnings by product lines may have to be disclosed.

Insider trading rules must be followed. People who are considered privy to inside information cannot profit from *short-swing* sales. Any time an officer, director, or 10-percent stockholder makes a buy and a sell within a six-month period, the profits must be surrendered to the corporation. No consideration is given to the purchase price of the actual stock sold. For example, if a company officer sells, at $10 per share, stock he had originally purchased at $20 per share, and then exercises his option to buy stock at $5 a share, he must return $5 per share to the company. (There was a sale at $10 and a purchase at $5 within a six month period.)

Rule 144

Officers, directors, and other persons holding unregistered shares of stock in a full-reporting company may sell stock under SEC Rule 144. There are strict limitations on the amount that can be sold and the manner in which the sale takes place. Your securities dealer can give you the details of Rule 144 if you let him know that you hold unregistered stock.

Insider information

Information known only to persons within the company cannot be disclosed to outsiders. Both the tipper and the tippee are liable for damages and penalties if unauthorized information that might affect the stock price is passed.

Public relations advisors

The company must follow all disclosure rules faithfully. If it lacks the manpower or the knowledge to do this it should hire a firm to make press releases on the company's behalf. The PR firm should be one with expertise in this field. In addition, the company's SEC attorney should be consulted regarding facts that may require disclosure.

The PR firm can also assist in the preparation of the annual report, proxy statements, and proxies, all of which must follow SEC guidelines.

It is hard to go back

There are many obstacles to going private once you are public. Few companies can pull it off. Do not go public unless the funds obtained can be put to good use within the company or unless there are shareholders who want to cash out. Evaluate the advantages and disadvantages carefully. Paper wealth can vanish overnight.

23
BUYING IN

One way to avoid the struggle of building a company from scratch is to buy one that has matured. It goes without saying that this requires both caution and courage as well as money and credibility. You need caution because that glittering balance sheet may be tinsel, courage because you are staking whatever you have accumulated on your own ability and credibility to convince the bank, the customers, and the employees that you can do the job.

Purchasing a profitable company

When you buy a successful business you do so more as an investor than as an entrepreneur. Normally you will pay top dollar because the owner will not be under pressure to sell. You will pay for earnings rather than assets, and the price will probably range between seven and fifteen times after-tax income. This may result in your paying for *good will*, which is the difference between the purchase price and the net worth.

Terms

Normally a business purchase requires a substantial downpayment, upwards of 30 percent. The balance can be paid off out of the profits. The seller is often willing to take a note for the unpaid balance, with the assets of the company pledged as collateral. The smaller the down payment, the greater the leverage. Slight increases in earnings can bring large returns.

Example of leverage

Suppose a business that earns $30,000 a year after taxes can be purchased for $50,000 down and a ten-year note for $200,000 at 8 percent interest. The first year's payment is $20,000 principal and $16,000 interest.

If the business earns the same as in prior years, it will have pretax earnings of approximately $60,000 from operations. The interest payment will reduce this to $44,000. After-tax earnings will be $22,000, leaving a $2,000 profit after the principal has been paid.

If the earnings are increased to $80,000, pretax, the after-tax income will be $32,000, leaving $12,000 after the principal payment. This is a sixfold increase in cash for a 33 percent increase in operating profit. The cash flow on the $50,000 investment is 24 percent, but because the business is paying itself off, the actual return is over 60 percent.

Obviously the leverage will work against you if profits fall. You might have to reduce your salary, (not included in the above computations) in order to make the payments on principal.

For most purchases to be worthwhile, the earnings of the business must be increased. Otherwise it might be better for the buyer to invest in stocks and keep on working for a salary. An exception is when the business is bought to ensure the new owner a lifetime job.

Buying a loss company

Maximum leverage can be obtained by buying a company that is losing money and then making it profitable. Loss companies cannot sell at multiples of earnings because there are no earnings. The price for such companies will range between the fair market value of the net assets and the distress-sale value.

Suppose that a company has $400,000 of annual sales, a net worth of $60,000, and is losing $15,000 yearly. A buyer might be able to purchase it for $40,000 or less. If he can then turn it around to where it produces an after-tax income of 10 percent, the business would have earned its purchase price in a single year. Its value would jump sixfold or so, because it would be based on earning power, not assets.

Such purchases are not uncommon. There are successful speculators who buy companies out of bankruptcy and sell them in a year or two at many times the purchase price.

Evaluating a company

Whether you buy a winner or a loser you must assure yourself that the company is as represented.

The financial statements are the company's public announcement of its self-appraisal. You must determine first whether they are correct and then what they really mean. If the statements have been audited by a CPA, then you can rely upon the numbers, if not the meaning behind them. But if the statements have not been audited, you should have an accountant investigate.

In addition to the financial statements you should examine the cash transactions of the company for the past three to five years. Primarily you should look for the amount of money the owners took out of the business for their personal use. The larger the sum, the more successful the business is apt to be. Cash earnings usually find their way into the founders' personal accounts. Other kinds of earnings are suspect.

Noncash profits

If the financial statements show large profits but little cash, such profits would be reflected in noncash items like land, building, equipment, and inventory. Such a condition might be understandable in a rapidly growing young company, but you would then have to question why it is up for sale.

Inventory

The great concealer of losses is inventory. Before you buy a company, inspect every inventory item and compare its real value with its book value. Do not delegate this task. You do it.

Each discrepancy you find should result in a lower purchase price.

I have seen many companies return rejected items to the stockroom and value them at cost. A little questioning of the employees may bring this to light. Employees will be reluctant to lie if questioned. They know you may become their new boss.

Production overruns and overbuys also have a way of finding themselves in inventory at full value. This is not necessarily a bad practice but it may be, particularly if the company builds to special orders.

Every item in the stockroom should have a specific, current use. When a design is changed, obsolete inventory should be purged from stock. It rarely is, however. The inventory records should reveal recent usage. If an item has not moved, it should be devalued.

I have even seen customer rejects returned to stock and carried on the books with the concurrence of the auditor, one of the big-eight accounting firms. Accountants can verify count and cost a lot easier than they can verify value.

Another questionable item is engineering costs. If the job is in process, engineering costs are legitimate. However, companies have a way of covering losses by keeping some of the engineering costs in inventory, on the premise that there will be future orders for the same product. This is not proper accounting, but it can often be slipped past the auditor.

Assets

Hiding losses in fixed assets is a little more difficult than concealing them in inventory, but it can be done. During production lulls, idle workers and engineers may be put to work constructing leasehold improvements or special tools and test equipment. The increase in asset value offsets the payroll expense. The value may be real but the accounting treatment distorts the true profit picture. Look for increases in assets that cannot be tied to purchase orders. These may represent false earnings.

The balance sheet

Lay out the balance sheets for the past three years side by side. Profits should show up in the difference between the accounts receivable and the accounts payable. If they do not, look for increases in cash or in distributed earnings. Otherwise, beware.

Owner dealings

If the balance sheet shows debts due from officers or owners, they may have been put there as window dressing. The owner should have been taking out a realistic salary. If his salary has been taken out in the form of loans, the profit has been distorted. On the other hand, if the owner has been taking out large sums it is a sign that the business is good, even if he gave notes in return.

All the answers are not on the balance sheets

Once you are satisfied that the company is a moneymaker, try to determine why. When the seller leaves, the customers may go with him. It may have been his talent that attracted customers or produced unique products. You must be in a position to replace that talent. You must also protect yourself from possible competition from him.

Use your attorney

There is no need to have an attorney present during your evaluation phase, but once you decide to buy you must get him involved. Make no agreement without him. He must protect you from unauthorized competition and hidden liabilities. Proceed on the assumption that the seller may know more than he has revealed, even to his own accountant, like a potential lawsuit or a product deficiency. Once you buy, those liabilities could become yours.

If you want to try a turnaround

You may find a company that is struggling to break even and know that it would thrive in your hands. If so, follow your intuition. You may never get a better opportunity.

What is it that you should look for? Sales. Particularly sales to loyal customers. If a company has customers in spite of broken delivery promises and poor quality, you know that it fills a need. If you can identify the cause of the problems, you may be able to achieve a turnaround in a few short months.

There are many companies that are held down only by poor management.

One common reason for good companies not making the grade is that the employees are taking advantage of a weak or unobserving boss. Restaurants, bars, service stations, and similar businesses require firm employee control for success. If you can provide it where the prior owner could not, you might have a bargain.

Look also for businesses with nonproductive activities and unprofitable projects. Simple surgery may provide quick success. Pet projects that bring psychological returns to scientists and engineers may be draining profits. So may ego-related products that should have been discontinued years ago. The other man's distress may be your opportunity.

Employee morale is essential

Often it is easy to cut costs and chop heads, but that is never the whole task. Employees who have worked for losers often become discouraged, cynical, and lethargic. You must bring them hope and the taste of success. Set simple goals at first and make sure they are met. Restore the self-confidence of the workers and managers alike. Give them pride in their accomplishments and faith in you.

Make changes quickly

New management often makes the mistake of promising that things will not change, then two or three months later instituting a major reorganization. The intent was correct, to quell fears, but the tactic is completely wrong.

Normally, employees dislike the thought of change, but when a new management takes over a distressed company they yearn for it. They want to see the company put on a sound footing.

Know what you plan to do before you make the purchase. Move quickly and make all the changes the first week. Tell the surviving employees what you expect of them. Elicit their advice. Implement it when it sounds reasonable.

Don't forget the financing

The purchase price is only part of the costs of a new business. Make certain that you have the funds available to back up your plans. Check with the banks. They may be so happy to see new management that they will agree to contribute to the company's salvation. Suppliers also may be willing to help by allowing stretched payments, particularly if you can show them how you will be a better customer.

And finally, the customers

Your customers will be nervous. They do not know you. Get out and talk to them. Tell them your plans. Work through your sales force as well. Let them be your advance men, carrying the word.

It won't be easy

Whether you start your own company or buy in, it is never easy. Running your own business requires competence and takes much personal effort. Success is never assured. You can fail in spite of all your good work. If you succeed it may be at too high a price. Yet you may achieve rewards beyond your wildest dreams. No matter what, it will be one hell of an adventure.

APPENDIX

CASH-FLOW FORECASTS

Before a cash-flow forecast can be prepared it is necessary to forecast new orders (bookings), sales (shipments or billings), and operating costs such as payroll and material purchased. To be conservative you must estimate costs on the high side, sales on the low side. You must also estimate collection time and payment time. Once again, collections must be estimated on the slow side. Because you have control over payments you may estimate them accurately.

Set up the time frame necessary to construct the cash forecasts. Shipments must be cued to the incoming order date. If your average delivery time is three months, an increase in sales will follow an increase in new orders by at least three months. The cost will build up almost immediately, however, as work goes into the job.

If you forecast a shipment 120 days after the incoming order, you may schedule the material receipt for 30 days and payment of the invoice in 60 days. Manpower will also build up quickly to reflect higher work loads, and payroll expenses are disbursed in the month they occur. Always schedule payroll expenses for the gross amount. Do not use the withholding tax as a source of financing. This can get you into serious problems if payroll taxes become overdue.

Lay out your forecast on a month-to-month basis. List your basic assumptions across the top of the page. Then list your receipts and disbursements. If you find you have a negative cash balance, you must be able to negotiate a bank loan. Insert the loan figure into the cash flow and make a second iteration that shows the receipt and the repayment of the loan. This is the document you take to the bank.

Show details

The more details you can provide, the better. If you can show exactly where the new orders are coming from and exactly what the shipments will be, by all means do so. List your payroll by person in a separate document. Where people must be hired, show how many and at what rate of pay. Use historical or estimated figures to determine the inputs of labor and material in the sales. Be prepared to justify the estimates. If the cash requirement comes from a build-up in actual backlog (rather than anticipated new orders) your expense figures should be conservative. The bank will not understand your inability to figure costs accurately.

See figure A-1 for an example of a cash-flow forecast that predicts the requirement for additional funds to finance a business surge.

COST ANALYSIS AND HOW IT CAN GO WRONG—
A CASE STUDY

Every large company has a cost accounting department that measures the profit performance of the products, divisions, and programs that make up the corporate sales. It issues reports, and executives often make the mistake of taking these reports at face value. This can lead to bad decisions.

The Trueline Machine Shop had two major programs. One was for a special, intricate valve that required 20 man-hours

Figure A-1/XYZ Company/Cash-Flow Forecast/(in thousands of dollars)

	Jan	Feb	Mar	Apr	May	Jun	Jul	Aug	Sep
New orders	50	70	100	60	80	80	70	80	80
Sales	60	60	60	60	70	100	80	80	80
Material received	18	18	20	35	30	30	25	25	25
Payroll (gross)	28	28	28	35	35	35	32	32	32
Cash on hand, BOM	10.5	13.7	14.9	13.1	5.9	29.7	7.5	3.9	5.3
Receipts:									
Accounts receivable	60	60	60	60	60	60	70	100	80
Bank loan					30				
Total receipts	60	60	60	60	90	60	70	100	80
Disbursements:									
Payroll	28	28	28	35	35	35	32	32	32
Payroll-related	5.6	5.6	5.6	7	7	7	6.4	6.4	6.4
Accounts payable	18	18	18	18	20	35	30	35	25
Bank repayment								20	
Tel. and tel.	.6	.6	.6	.6	.6	.6	.6	.6	.6
Travel and enter.	1	1	1	1	1	1	1	1	1
Occupancy costs	2.6	2.6	2.6	2.6	2.6	2.6	2.6	2.6	2.6
Acctg. and legal		2	1	1					
Petty cash	1	1	1	1	1	1	1	1	1
Local taxes			4						
Total disbursements	56.8	58.8	61.8	66.2	67.2	82.2	73.6	98.6	68.6
Cash flow (deficit)	3.2	1.2	(1.8)	(6.2)	22.8	(22.2)	(3.6)	.4	11.4
									16.7 EOM

of machining per unit. It was made from an inexpensive steel casting. At the end of the fabrication, the unit was painted, packed, and shipped.

The second program was for a relatively simple microwave assembly that took only 4 man-hours of shop labor but had a number of subcontracted processing steps. Pieces were machined, then sent out for dip-braizing. Upon return they were straightened and some additional machine cuts were made. Once again they were sent out for dip-braizing to an added section, then back to the shop for holes, then out for heat treating and silver plating.

In the machine shop there were 15 persons charged to indirect functions, including a factory manager, 2 foremen, several planners, a buyer, 2 expediters, 2 stockroom clerks, and 3 inspectors.

These overhead people serviced a shop with 25 machinists. All the work was bid competitively. Because the company was barely breaking even, the company president asked his CPA firm for a cost analysis of the two programs.

One further bit of information is needed. The company was using a Department of Defense-approved accounting system whereby manufacturing overhead was allocated as a function of direct labor.

Here is a copy of the accountant's report:

	Valve	Microwave Assembly	Total
Units	175 @ $240	200 @ $130	
Sales	$42,000	26,000	$68,000
Direct labor	20,000	5,000	25,000
Mfg. overhead @ 80%	16,000	4,000	20,000
Mat'l. & subcontracts	1,000	10,000	11,000
Mfg. costs	37,000	19,000	56,000
G & A @ 20%	7,400	3,800	11,200
Total costs	44,400	22,800	67,200
Pretax profit (loss)	(2,400)	3,200	800

The accountant stated that of the two product lines, the

microwave assembly was more desirable because it was realizing a profit of $16 per unit (12 percent), whereas the valve was losing $14 a unit. The accountant recommended getting more microwave assembly and less valve business. The president told the sales department to lower the unit price of the microwave assembly $10 each and raise the unit price of the valve $14 each, hoping to increase sales of the assembly and cut losses on the valve.

His strategy worked beautifully. Sales of the valve dropped from 175 units to 100 units and sales of the microwave assembly rose from 200 units to 400. Total sales rose from $67,200 to over $73,000. The payroll dropped slightly because not so many machinists were needed. The overhead people stayed at the previous number because most of their work had been spent on processing the microwave assembly. In fact, one machinists was switched to production control rather than being laid off. The president was delighted. He had higher sales, a better mix, and a lower payroll. What more could he ask? Then the results came in from accounting.

	Valve	Microwave Assembly	Total
Units	100 @ $254	400 @ $120	
Sales	$25,400	48,000	$73,400
Direct labor	12,000	10,000	22,000
Mfg. overhead @ 95%	11,500	9,500	21,000
Mat'l. & subcontracts	700	20,000	20,700
Mfg. costs	24,200	39,500	63,700
G & A @ 17%	4,500	6,700	11,200
Total costs	28,700	46,200	74,900
Pretax profit (loss)	(3,300)	1,800	(1,500)

The result came as a shock. Both products had done worse than before! The accountant pointed at the valve and said it was the loser. Give it some more of the same medicine, he advised.

The president was not to be taken in, however. If a little does not work, a lot may be disastrous. He did an about-face and lowered the price of the valve to $220 and raised the price of the microwave assembly to $150. As a result, he sold 230 valves and 150 assemblies for a total of $73,100, the same as the previous month but with what appeared to be an unfavorable mix. The results now looked like this:

	Microwave		
	Valve	Assembly	Total
Units	230 @ $220	150 @ $150	
Sales	$50,600	22,500	$73,100
Direct labor	27,600	3,800	31,400
Mfg. overhead @ 60%	16,600	2,400	19,000
Mat'l. & subcontracts	1,500	7,500	9,000
Mfg. costs	45,700	13,700	59,400
G & A @ 19%	8,800	2,400	11,220
Total costs	$54,500	16,100	70,600
Pretax profit (loss)	(3,900)	6,400	2,500

As you can see, the results made very little sense. The more money lost on the valves, the more made on the microwave assembly.

The president became convinced that it was the accounting system that was weak, not the valves. The out-of-pocket costs to make the valves were $29,100 for sales of $50,600, leaving a total of $20,500 to pay other costs. Similarly, the microwave assembly contributed only $11,200. What's more, of the $19,000 in overhead costs, over two-thirds were spent on the microwave assembly. All the president had had to do was ask for a pro forma operating statement before he acted. He would have seen the results before he made his price changes. That is what you should do. Be a little cautious when the accountant tells you you have a loser on your hands. Products that just perk away, day after day, without disturbing anyone or anything, are rarely losers.

TOOLS OF MARKETING

Just in case you think you are doing everything that can be done in your marketing effort, I have prepared this checklist for you.

KNOWLEDGE

Do you know your market?

Have you a file of published market reports and forecasts?

Did your company generate its own forecast of the market?

Are customers asked about their future requirements?

Are the underlying economic causes of the market condition understood?

Do you get market information from your reps and salesmen?

Do you know your customers?

Do you know what programs each has, and whether he is funded?

Have you a history of his past procurements?

Do you know his buying habits and evaluation criteria?

Do you know his organization and how it works?

Do you know all the key people?

Do you know your competitors?

Do you know how much each sells and to whom?

Do you know the strengths and weaknesses of his product?

Do you know what programs he has in house?

Do you have copies of his price lists?

Do you know how he stands with each of his customers?

Do you know his financial strength?

Have you copies of his annual reports and Form 10Ks?

Do you know his goals?

EXECUTION

How well have you planned your sales?

Do you have a marketing plan?

Do you have a capture plan?

Do you understand the market needs?

Are you in close contact with the customers?

Have you defined your key accounts?

Do you know who has money to spend?

Have you made a sales forecast?

Have you communicated with everyone who will be involved?

Have you sold the factory on your plan?

How well is the company exposed?

Do you advertise regularly?

Do you have brochures and catalogs?

Do you have a direct mail program?

Do you have application notes on your product's use?

Do your salesmen have a written manual?

Does your company get free advertising through product releases?

Is your company in the news?

Are company executives on civic boards or national committees?

How well is the product defined?

Do you understand its basic benefits?

Is the performance defined?

Do you have a record of product reliability?

How does it compare with competition in price and delivery?

Is the company behind the product?

Does it respond when queried?

Does it meet its delivery promises?

Does it back up its warranty?

Does it back its salesmen's word?

Will it help a customer in need?

Can the company back its claims with facts?
Does it have test data and test reports?

Does it have specification approvals?

Does it have customer endorsements?

Does it have reliability data? Samples? Photos?

Can you invite customers into the factory?

Will they be impressed?

Do you have a good delivery performance record?

What will the bank say about the company?

Do your salesmen work effectively?
Do they schedule their calls?

Do they know their customers?

Do they know your product?

Do they have samples and price lists?

Can they give ball-park estimates for price and delivery?

Do they hit all the bases? Purchasing, engineering, manufacturing, etc?

Do they entertain properly? The right people?

Will they call on the factory when they are in trouble?

Do they get many requirements?

Can they close?

Do they ask for the order?

Does the factory respond?
Are all sales and customer inquiries answered promptly?

Is the customer notified at the first sign of a delay?

Does the company have a late-order status report?

Will the company bend on prices?

Will the company make special orders?

Does the quality control manager check with customers?

Is the marketing effort evaluated?

Is the bookings report checked against forecasts?

Is there a lost business report?

Is there a lost customer report?

Are new accounts targeted and results recorded?

Are the price recommendations justified by subsequent events?

Is the company capturing a greater share of the market?

Are sales growing in accordance with the plan?

Is the advertising effective? How is it evaluated?

Is management involved?

Does the president know what is happening in sales?

Does he help sell?

Does he insist on company support?

Do the other executives know what is going on?

Do they help sell? Insist on sales support?

Is the company marketing oriented?

Does everyone consider things from the customer standpoint?